CHASING
THE
VISION

LELAND EDWARDS
with RON WILLIAMS

CREATION
HOUSE
A STRANG COMPANY

Foursquare Media

CHASING THE VISION by Leland Edwards with Ron Williams
Published by Creation House
A Strang Company
600 Rinehart Road
Lake Mary, Florida 32746
www.creationhouse.com

Unless otherwise noted, all Scripture quotations are from the Revised Standard Version of the Bible. Copyright © 1946, 1952, 1971 by the Division of Christian Education of the National Council of the Churches of Christ in the USA. Used by permission.

Scripture quotations marked KJV are from the King James Version of the Bible.

Cover design by Terry Clifton

Library of Congress Control Number: 2006926084
International Standard Book Number: 1-59979-019-X

First Edition

06 07 08 09 10 — 987654321
Printed in the United States of America

◁ Acknowledgments

I HAVE DISCOVERED THAT putting one's memoirs into print is no easy task. I am deeply grateful for those who took a special interest in the formation of this book.

My good friend and golf partner, Doug Cobb, of Ridgecrest, California, reviewed the original drafts of my stories.

I asked Dr. Ron Williams, former missionary to Asia, former editor of the *Foursquare World ADVANCE Magazine*, pastor, teacher, and recognized author to formulate the material into an acceptable text. My main request was: "In the end, please let it sound like me." My wife and I love the style and agree that it does. Without Ron, this book would not have been completed.

I am grateful to Wanda Brackett, of our Foursquare central office, whose editorial eye for detail and grammar has greatly enhanced the text. She has been a considerable help.

Then there is my wife, Barbara, whose encouragement has been beyond words. As I wrote the stories, both of us enjoyed reliving many of those never-to-be-forgotten experiences from our many years of ministry.

Above all, thanks be to God, for without His grace and mercy in the lives of people, there would be no stories to tell. To Him be glory and honor!

—LELAND EDWARDS
MARCH 2005

➤ Contents

THERE IS NOT a handbook on success published today that doesn't emphasize the need for "vision." It has become fundamental as a concept if anyone would realize personal or corporate success. So it is particularly gratifying to be presented with a book like this which focuses on "vision," but carries the matter to dimensions that transcend a mere quest for momentary market gains, power leveraging, or economic achievement. Far more, here is an adventure story—a true one, compelling in its significance, as it is a success story of enormous and timeless proportions.

I was first introduced to the elements of this book more than thirty years ago. Today, it is hard to describe the delight I feel, not only that it is being presented in a way that will preserve its excitement, inspiration, and message for the future, but that I am privileged to introduce you to the book and the author.

I have known Leland Edwards and his wife, Barbara, for more than four decades. I met them, in fact, just after they returned to the United States from their many years as missionaries in Panama. If the test of a life well-lived is the measure of the joys and benefits an individual or couple brings to others, while tasting much of those things themselves, then Lee and Barb are the epitome of success.

Leland and Barbara are one of the most remarkable couples I have ever known. They have demonstrated that rare possibility of two people with remarkable leadership and talent, *both* delivering on the maximum of their potential, and *each* evidencing a total commitment to one another. Neither their home nor their marriage suffered from the fact they were both full-time missionaries serving international schedule demands, and tirelessly faithful in caring for the multinational task placed under their charge.

The vision they served was ignited like a torch in the generation of Leland's parents, then taken up and advanced by Lee and Barb. They modeled the finest in servant-leadership, and have given their entire lives to serving Christ, His Kingdom, and His people—often in some of the most out-of-the-way places on the globe.

Their self-sacrifice is clearly evidenced throughout the following pages of their memoirs. By anyone's standards, the work they did as missionaries is remarkable. Adding to that extraordinary service is the cheerfulness with which they rendered it. When they faced hardships and challenges, they embraced them as adventures. When they faced suffering, they met it with joy and patience that were truly Christlike.

Leland had the marvelous benefit of being reared by parents who were missionaries—pioneer missionaries. Leland grew up seeing God perform amazing miracles as the Foursquare gospel began to spread throughout the nation of Panama. After his parents retired, he had the unique honor and pleasure of being able to assume the supervision of the work they had started. And he carried the banner superbly, preserving for future generations the legacy that began with his parents' obedience to a heavenly vision.

On a personal level, Leland and Barbara are people of unsurpassed warmth and generosity. They are genuine—with them, what you see is what you get. I am sure that their children and grandchildren would say the same thing. In fact, the Edwards' children and grandchildren, who are all serving the Lord today, are testimonials to the fact that Leland and Barbara practiced what they preached.

I know you will enjoy these pages. They are more than memoirs—they are the incarnation of Christ's life in and through human beings. I believe you will not only be refreshed, but will find faith and spiritual dynamism rise in your soul as you read of miracles that inevitably occur where that kind of "recurrent incarnation" takes place. It is what the apostle Paul described as "Christ in you—the hope of glory!" (See Colossians 1:27.)

May that glory multiply in and through us all!

—JACK W. HAYFORD, PRESIDENT
INTERNATIONAL CHURCH OF THE FOURSQUARE GOSPEL
LOS ANGELES, CALIFORNIA

I N 1927 AN elderly man living in an interior province of Panama earnestly asked God to span the miles and send someone to that nation with the gospel. He recorded his prayer in his personal journal.

That same day, three thousand miles away, in Los Angeles, California, a middle-aged man, while in prayer, received a vision from the Lord, vividly showing him the man in Panama who had made that request.

The rest is Foursquare history, telling the story of what led up to that day, and what happened afterward, all because of one man's dedication and that of his family to "chase the vision," and do the will of God.

A few years ago I decided to begin writing my memoirs, mainly with my grandchildren in mind. I wanted them and their descendants, should the Lord tarry, to have the story about how and why I was taken, as an eight-year-old, from California to Panama. I spent the next thirty-two years of my life in that nation, and I wanted to leave them with some of the highlights of those years. I began writing stories and e-mailing them to our children and grandchildren. Those stories were related to others; before long, the list of recipients was much larger than I could have imagined.

When I speak in churches, I include the stories of actual experiences I have had ministering in other countries. At the conclusion of the services, people come, inquiring when I will write a book about those happenings. Thus, I decided the time had arrived to give it a try.

—LELAND B. EDWARDS

◄ A Little Bit About Me

ON AUGUST 15, 1511, Spanish explorers established their first city in the Americas in Panama. On the same date in 1914, the Panama Canal opened to seagoing traffic. Exactly five years later, I, Leland Edwards, was born in San Jose, California. Eight years later, my family would move to Panama, which would be my home for the next thirty-two years.

My first six years were spent in Paradise Valley—just three miles from downtown Morgan Hill. Our family lived on a prune and walnut orchard. When I was old enough to start school, I walked to the Machado School, one-and-a-half miles away, to start first grade. It was a two-room school, with four grades in each room and one teacher for each room. However, after only a few weeks, we moved to Los Angeles so Dad and Mother could attend the International Institute of Foursquare Evangelism to prepare for the ministry. Arriving in Los Angeles, I did the rest of the school year in Logan Street School.

As far back as I can remember, our whole family participated in what was called "The Family Altar." Before anyone left for work, and generally right after breakfast, all five of us read a chapter from the Bible together. Each one would pray, and our entire family would recite the Lord's Prayer. Often, one of my parents would read from a Bible storybook. My grandfather would tell me a Bible story without naming the person it was about, and then ask me to tell him whom he was talking about. I remember the moment when I was five years old that I told my mother I wanted to receive Jesus as my Savior. I knelt at her knee and gave my heart to the Lord. It was a genuine salvation experience.

Our family schedule included Sunday school, morning worship, and evening evangelistic service each Sunday. It also included prayer meeting on Wednesday nights where the whole congregation, after a short Bible teaching from the pastor, got down on their knees and prayed aloud. Often, someone received the baptism of the Holy Spirit. People prayed for each other. Men and women, boys and girls were healed of their illnesses.

On Saturday evenings, our family took part in the street meeting in the center of town. On Sunday afternoons, we children were asked to tell one of our parents what the minister had taught in his message that morning. I was required to memorize verses from the Bible.

When we moved down to Los Angeles, the schedule for church attendance increased. Services were held every night in the main auditorium of Angelus Temple with capacity crowds. Divine healing services were conducted each Wednesday afternoon and Saturday night. I can still remember the many miracles as God healed sick and afflicted bodies in those services. Thursday night was the water baptismal service. At the age of seven, I was baptized in water by Sister McPherson.

During the second year of Bible college, Dad and Mother were invited to preach in some of the branch churches in different parts of the city. People seemed to think that I had a good singing voice, so from time to time I sang a solo before the sermon. Two of my favorite songs were "I'm a Child of the King" and "There's Going to Be a Meeting in the Air." I also sang a couple of times in Angelus Temple, each time standing on a chair on the platform. I must confess I was reluctant to sing before more than five thousand people, so my parents bribed me by giving me a twenty-five cent toy of my choice.

When my family arrived in Panama, before disembarking at the port of Balboa, we had to be vaccinated against smallpox. A nurse did the vaccination by scratching a small area on my upper left arm with a needle and then putting a drop of the vaccine in the wound. The vaccine produced a sore that took a few days to heal and left a scar about half an inch in diameter. The law required a new vaccination every three years for all residents until the 1950s, when smallpox had virtually been eradicated worldwide.

Although we lived in Panama City and not in the Canal Zone, I attended the U. S. government schools in the Zone from the third grade on, graduating from Balboa High School in 1937. I liked school: my studies, fellow students, and school activities, including sports. Track was my favorite. The records I set for the 440- and 880-yard runs stood for twelve years.

We lived in a rented two-story house at the very end of Mariano Arosemena Street. The solid jungle started just the other side of our fence. I made friends with all of the kids who lived in the immediate area and with some of their parents. Most of them spoke only Spanish, so I quickly picked up the language mainly by my association with them and the people attending our church services.

Our home was sometimes termed "The Edwards Hotel." In those days international air travel was not yet heard of. Practically all ships between North America and South America made port in Panama. Over the years we had many missionary visitors from different church movements in our home; they needed a place to stay until their ship would arrive to take them to their destination. I listened to many of their experiences: times of success and times of disappointment.

One time the Clarence Jones family arrived and stayed a few days. They were quite discouraged, having visited several of the Latin American countries while looking for the ideal conditions to carry out their calling from the Lord. God was leading them to start a gospel radio station. One morning, in a time of family devotions, Dad gave them a promise from the Bible. They took that for themselves and, instead of giving up and returning to the United States, they went south to Ecuador and found just the right conditions to establish the Voice of the Andes radio station, HCJB. For many decades this station broadcast the gospel to the world in many different languages.

As I look back on my childhood and teen years, I am so thankful to the Lord for the way my parents raised me. They believed in and practiced obedience. When I was disobedient, and sometimes after spanking or scolding me, my mother would get out the Bible and read to me from the Word, explaining what God had to say about the matter. My parents loved me, and I loved them. They were a real covering for me through all of those growing-up years.

One day in April 1937, when I came home from school, there was a letter waiting for me with unexpected news. It stated that I had been appointed a Foursquare Crusader Missionary, and my salary would be twenty-five dollars a month! In 1934, the Crusader Youth movement of the Foursquare Church in the United States started supporting MKs (missionary kids) in their late teens or early adult years who felt called to be missionaries. All along I had felt in my spirit that God wanted me to be a missionary even though, when I was asked, I replied that I wanted to be an aeronautical engineer. I liked airplanes and someday hoped to fly.

After reading the letter and handing it to my parents to read, they asked what I was going to do. I replied, "I'll do my best to be a good one." (Months later, my father told me, "If you don't produce better preachers and teachers than yourself, you will be a failure.") I was seventeen at the time and already had been preaching for two years. In June of that year, as soon as I finished high school, I gave myself to the ministry as God opened the doors. God surely made a way for me. But that was not all!

Before Christmas of 1939, my parents and I started our furlough by taking a fruit company ship from Panama to Los Angeles. The ship made a stop in Quepos, Costa Rica, where it took on its cargo of bananas. As the boat docked in Los Angeles Harbor, we could see Harold Chalfant, Roy Bell, and Karl and Leona Williams on the pier to meet us. It was a cold winter night and the Williamses had brought a welcome gift for each of us:

for my mother a flannel nightgown, and for Dad and me flannel pajamas. The next morning we attended the service at Angelus Temple. That night we left by train for Morgan Hill to spend Christmas with family.

The three of us were delegates at the annual convention of the International Church of the Foursquare Gospel, held at Angelus Temple during the first days of 1940. Afterward we teamed up with Dr. and Mrs. Sidney Correll to conduct three missionary conferences.

The first conference took place at the Burbank, California, Foursquare Church. For me, the big event of the three-day meetings took place near the conclusion of the Sunday morning service. After finishing his message and telling of things God had done in Panama, Dad gave an altar call for those who would give their lives in ministry wherever God would lead them. Several came forward, and one of them was a very beautiful young blonde lady. The Lord spoke to me, "There is your mate for life." I didn't know her name or anything about her. Many months later, in fact after we were married, I learned that, as they were going home from church that Sunday morning, her mother said to her father, "Someday Barbara is going to marry Leland Edwards." He replied, "You must be crazy."

A few weeks later, I spoke at a Crusader Youth rally in the North Hollywood Foursquare Church. Barbara attended along with her parents, Larry and Gladys Noyes, both graduates of LIFE Bible College. After the meeting, I took Barbara out on our first date to an ice cream parlor. Barbara had accepted Jesus as her Savior when she was five years old. She was now seventeen years of age and attending Burbank High School in the final semester of her senior year. At the same time, she was attending LIFE Bible College at night. I was a member of the senior class of LIFE Bible College that spring semester, and Barbara was my guest to the junior/senior banquet at Knott's Berry Farm. We had another date or two before school was over for the summer.

Unfortunately, during the summer of 1940 my furlough from

missionary ministry in Panama came to an end. My father had already returned to Panama and, on July 3, my mother and I boarded a Japanese ship to return to Panama. Our departure was delayed a day, and Barbara and her parents came to the Los Angeles harbor and found that we were still there. They took us out for a ride. Barbara and I were dropped off at the Pike in Long Beach. We rode the rollercoaster several times and were flung around on a few other rides. Back at the ship, when we said our good-byes, I told her to be sure to write to me. She replied, "You write to me first."

During the next thirteen months, we kept the mail service busy with letters sent by airmail. At Christmas I received a very nice card from her and in it she wrote: "The girl who gets to marry you will be very lucky." A few weeks later I wrote to her, asking her to marry me. When the letter arrived at her home, she was out at Johannesburg in the California desert helping in services in the Foursquare Church. Her parents drove out to Johannesburg with my letter containing the special request. Of course, she said, "Yes!" After Barbara had consented to marry me, I sent money to a friend, Guy Martin, a student in LIFE Bible College, asking him to purchase an engagement ring in my name for Barbara. Later I found out that she convinced Guy to take her with him to pick it out!

In June of that year, Colonel Arden Bennett, head of the Civil Service Office of the Panama Canal, came to our door and asked me to accept employment in his office. He had found the Lord under my mother's ministry and needed help with some special work. I worked there for three months, which gave me the extra money to send to Barbara for her fare to come to Panama on an American President Line ship. She arrived on a Sunday night, and a week later, on the morning of August 31, 1941, we were married in the Panama City Foursquare Church. In fact, we were married twice that day. At that time, Panamanian law did not recognize a marriage conducted in a non-Catholic church. Since I was temporarily employed by the Panama Canal, I was eligible to get our marriage license in the Canal Zone. So that morning Dad drove Barbara and me from Panama City to Ancon in the Canal Zone. He married us as we sat in the back seat of the car (yes, that was the official—legal—ceremony!), and then he drove us to the church ceremony. I must admit that I preached that night in the very church where my "Babe," Barbara, and I had tied the knot.

Over the years, sixty-three as of this writing, God has blessed our ministry and our home. He has filled our lives with love, faithfulness, and so many blessings. God gave us two wonderful sons, both born in Panama. They, their wives, their children, and their children's spouses are all following the Lord. In fact, all of them are members of Foursquare churches.

History is best written from a "firsthand" perspective. Long before there were books written regarding missionary strategy and missionary family life, I watched my parents discern God's will and leave their native country to preach the gospel in another country. I observed how they balanced learning a new culture, starting a new church movement, and at the same time, raising their family on the foundations of faith. It is a legacy to the Edwards family, and to our Foursquare Church in the United States and in Panama. It is a story that had to be told, and I am delighted to share it with you.

◁ Continuing to the Fourth Generation

ARTHUR EDWARDS, MY father, was born in Spring Valley, Minnesota, on March 17, 1881. His father, Frank V. Edwards, was the junior partner of the bank in that town and an elder in the local Congregational church. His father-in-law was the senior partner of the bank and also Grand Master of the Masonic Lodge in Minnesota. In addition to being leading citizens, Frank and his wife, Kate, were dedicated members of the church. Frank was the teacher of the adult Sunday school class. Both he and Kate were very much involved in social activities in the community. He was a personal friend of the Mayo brothers, original founders of the world-renowned Mayo Clinic in Rochester, Minnesota. He would often meet them at the train station when they visited Spring Valley, and he would take them in his carriage to people in urgent physical need.

As far back as the eighteenth century, the Congregational church in the time of Jonathan Edwards was a strong fundamental and evangelical movement. God had used this wonderful church in spiritual awakenings in the American colonies and later in the United States of America. However, over the years, there had been a gradual falling away. Toward the end of the last decade of the 1800s, a new pastor came to the Congregational church in Spring Valley. He was what they called a "modernist." He doubted the virgin birth of Jesus Christ, and omitted the blood of Christ from his theology. My grandfather, Frank, continued to teach the Sunday school class, but refused to attend the regular church services in protest of the teaching of the new pastor. Yet, in their home, the family was very consistent in daily devotions and said grace at each meal. Arthur grew up in a rich

Christian atmosphere and heritage.

Following his studies at the University of Minnesota, Arthur worked in the family bank until 1906 when the Edwards family moved to California. They settled in the town of Morgan Hill, just south of San Jose, a short time before the great San Francisco earthquake. In their new community, they again entered the banking business. The area was emerging as a farming community: mostly prune and walnut orchards. They later sold the bank, bought land in nearby Paradise Valley, and opened a general merchandise store in Morgan Hill. Since there was no Congregational church within miles, they joined the local Methodist church. There, Arthur met a young lady schoolteacher, Edith Breton.

Edith was originally from South Dakota, had belonged to the Methodist Church from early childhood, and was a graduate of Stanford University and San Jose Normal College. She testified of a born-again experience from an early age. Edith and Arthur, who later became my parents, were married on June 10, 1911, in Saratoga, California. They lived in San Francisco and later in Scotia, California, where Arthur was the head paymaster for the Pacific Lumber Company. After a few years, they returned to Morgan Hill to live on their Paradise Valley ranch tending to their prune and walnut orchards.

One Sunday morning the local dentist and teacher of the church's adult Bible class announced that he would be absent the next Lord's Day. He also announced that Arthur Edwards would teach the class in his stead. He made the announcement without approval from my dad who immediately objected, but to no avail. As the days of the week went by, Dad tried to get others to teach the class, but no one was willing. The assignment weighed heavily on him. Finally, with only one day left, he rose from the breakfast table, harnessed the team of horses, and went into the orchard to work. Suddenly, he stopped the team and in desperation cried out, "God, if you are really God, please reveal Yourself to me. How can I give to that class tomorrow what I do not possess myself?"

God began answering his prayer almost immediately. My dad became so ill that he was hardly able to return home. Mother phoned the family doctor in San Jose, but he was out on another case. She then called a doctor in nearby Gilroy. He came and diagnosed that my dad had typhoid fever and promised to send medicine the next day.

That night Dad had a vision. In the vision a man came riding into his bedroom on a black horse and told him to climb up on the horse behind him. They rode along the foothills ten miles to Gilroy and into the office of the doctor, who had a vial in his hand, mixing medicine for Dad to take. The man warned him, "If you take that, you will die." The next day, an assistant to that doctor came with the medicine, but Dad refused to open his mouth. Mother called their regular doctor and he came to the house. He immediately said that her husband must be taken to the hospital. An ambulance was called and my father was taken to San Jose with double pneumonia.

There, Dad had an experience that would change the rest of his life. On what was supposed to have been my dad's deathbed, God spoke to him through another vision. In this vision, my dad's soul was taken from his body and it descended into hell where he suffered indescribable torment. It should be said that the pastor of the church my parents were attending taught that hell was not a place of literal torment, but simply the bad times in this life. Then my father was taken to the door of heaven, with his back turned to the entrance. God showed him His Word:

> And many of those who sleep in the dust of the earth shall awake, some to everlasting life, and some to shame and everlasting contempt. And those who are wise shall shine like the brightness of the firmament; and those who turn many to righteousness, like the stars for ever and ever.
> —Daniel 12:2–3

He was also shown the heavens, with the predominant bright stars and the great Milky Way, with its millions of stars that are so difficult to distinguish one from the other. God said to him: *Those represent the vast multitude that will barely make it into heaven, having done little to turn people to Me. Now you know there is a hell, and now you know there is a heaven. Now you know there is a God, and, if you are willing, you may turn around and look upon the glory and beauty of heaven. But if you do, you will have to stay.* Dad replied, "God, if I enter heaven now I would enter as a naked soul. I have never won anyone to You. Please give me one more chance to live. I'll give the rest of my life to telling others about You."

Within a very short time my dad was back home and well. He would never forget the promise he had made to the Lord. He left the hospital as a new creature in Christ Jesus. It was not long before he organized a small group to conduct street meetings each Saturday night in front of the town's pool hall, next door to the bank, which the family had owned for several years. The Edwards home also became a meeting place for Bible studies and prayer meetings. The ministry of my dad, Arthur F. Edwards, began in 1920, and it has continued through the second, third, and now the fourth generations of the Edwards family.

In 1921, my parents attended a tent campaign in San Jose, conducted by Aimee Semple McPherson. For an entire month she preached three times a day to well over six thousand people in each service. When the time came for her to pray for the sick, Dad joined the choir to get a closer look. He saw miracles happen. He saw sight instantly given to a blind man, to the amazement of the crowd. A woman's goiter was melted instantly in answer to prayer. Arthritic joints were made well, and broken bones were instantly healed. More than one thousand two hundred people within a fifty-mile radius of San Jose reported being healed and registered their healings and their addresses with the pastor of the First Baptist Church, who had invited the evangelist to San Jose. Hundreds more from farther away also had been touched by the Master. For the first time, my parents learned that Jesus was not only the Savior, but also the Baptizer with the Holy Spirit, our Healer, and the King who was coming again very soon to receive all those who had accepted the gospel message through the ages to be with Him forever.

The following year my parents attended Sister McPherson's campaign in Oakland, California. For the first time, Sister McPherson identified the four cardinal doctrines of her message as "The Foursquare Gospel": 1.) Jesus Christ is the Savior; 2.) Jesus is the Baptizer with the Holy Spirit; 3.) Jesus is the Healer; and 4.) Jesus is the Coming King. Dad and Mother decided this was the message they wanted to preach and teach to others.

As a family, we drove down to Los Angeles to attend the inaugural service in Angelus Temple on January 1, 1923. When Sister McPherson went on the air with her radio station, KFSG, a few months later, my father purchased the best radio receiver available so that he could listen to the services from Angelus Temple. I was just a small boy, but I especially looked forward to each Thursday night when we could hear the splashes as people were baptized in water. Family and friends gathered in our home to listen to Sister McPherson preach. Dad also began holding street meetings in the town of Hollister, about twenty miles away. As a result, a new church was pioneered.

"Sister," as she was affectionately known, announced that she would be starting a Bible institute to train missionaries, pastors, evangelists, and teachers. My parents realized they needed training to be able to have an effective soul-winning ministry. In the spring of 1925, there was a strong desire in their hearts to formally study God's Word to prepare to serve the Lord. In order to have enough money to move to Los Angeles to complete a two-year course of study, they decided to wait one more year. Dad would plant vegetables between the rows of trees in his orchard.

Before retiring for the night, Dad made out an order for the seeds, wrote the check for full payment, and sealed the envelope for mailing the next morning. That night he saw a vision. In the vision, he had harvested the vegetables, and the truck was fully loaded. He had backed the truck up to the dock of the wholesale market in San Jose, waiting for the early dawn opening to sell the entire load. Sitting in the cab, he suddenly heard a strange noise. Looking to the right, he saw a group of firefighters pulling an old fire engine, like those seen in museums. They were so tired their tongues were hanging out of their mouths. As they went by, he hollered at them, "Where are you going?" They replied, "To Balboa." Dad looked to the south, and saw the fire of God's judgment fall upon that place. *They will never make it in time,* he thought. The vision ended. He asked God for the meaning of the vision. The Lord was emphatic: if his truck had been empty, he could have put the fire engine with the firefighters on it, and they would have made it in time. He realized God was telling him to not delay preparing for the ministry.

But that name, *Balboa,* where was that place? Dad got out a large map of the world and from Morgan Hill, California, just south of San Jose, he looked to Balboa Beach, California, outside of Los Angeles, where his aunt was carrying on a gospel work. But that was not the place. Reaching much farther to the south, he put his finger on the map saying, "The fire fell down this way." Under his finger was the name *Balboa,* the port of entry on the Pacific side of Panama. Immediately he felt within himself the welling up of the Holy Spirit, *Yes, that is the nation to which you are called to take the gospel.*

When he informed my mother, a crisis occurred in the Edwards' household. "Arthur (when she used that name it had to be serious!), you should have thought about being a missionary when we were young. We are now in our mid-forties; we have our family and our home." But Dad was eager to obey God and talked to his father about the problem. Grandpa told him to pray that God would also call my mother. A few days later, as Mother was alone praying in the livingroom, God gave her a vision. Looking out the large living room window she saw a lady sitting under the oak tree in the front yard, dressed in the typical country dress of Panama. Now, she knew for certain that God had also called her to that country.

3

◁ To Los Angeles, Then to Panama

SOON AFTER THE prune and walnut harvest was over in
early fall 1925, my father and mother, Arthur and Edith
Edwards; my brother, Donald; my sister, Barbara; and I
left the ranch in Paradise Valley and moved to Los Angeles. We
arrived in time for Mom and Dad to start their classes in the
1925 fall semester of the International Institute of Foursquare
Evangelism at Angelus Temple. The name of the institute was
later changed to Lighthouse of International Foursquare Evangelism, or LIFE Bible College.

Three of our cousins moved south with us to attend the
institute: Frank, Bernice, and Roberta Thompson. Together we
rented a house on Logan Street, in the Echo Park area, about a
block from Angelus Temple. All of us attended Angelus Temple.
Services were held morning, afternoon, and night on Sundays
and also every night of the week. There were also special divine
healing services on Wednesday afternoons and Saturday nights.
On the weekdays, morning services were held in the "500 Room"
of the temple. To find seats in the evening services, people had
to be at the doors of the temple before they opened, because the
auditorium, which seated five thousand, three hundred, filled to
capacity in a matter of minutes.

I remember well many of the sermons that Aimee Semple
McPherson preached on Sunday nights—all vividly illustrated. The altar calls were enormous. The large altar space in
front of the platform would be filled, several rows deep, with
people who had lifted their hands in response when the call
was given. They stood to their feet, even from the first and
second balconies, and made their way down the aisles to the

altar to receive Jesus as their Savior.

On Wednesday afternoons, there was a solid line of ambulances parked in front of the temple, stretching from the corner of Lemoyne Street to the alley on Glendale Boulevard. The ambulances brought sick people from hospitals and homes. Many of these men and women were beyond the help of medical science. The entire space in front of the platform was filled with these people lying on stretchers. During prayer for the sick, many would be healed instantly and would get up from their stretchers. Many of the ambulances would return to their original destinations empty.

During the summer of 1926 we drove to Crescent City, in northern California. My parents rented the city hall for nightly services. Shortly after we arrived, a crisis occurred in the local hospital. A boy had just had a tonsillectomy and was hemorrhaging. The doctor and nurses were unable to stop the flow of blood and the parents were frantic. Dad and Mother were asked to go to the hospital and pray for him. They laid hands on the child in the name of Jesus, and instantly the bleeding stopped. News of this miracle spread quickly, and night after night the city hall, which was a storefront filled with benches, was packed with people. That was the beginning of the Foursquare Church in Crescent City.

After that evangelistic campaign, our family returned to the ranch in Morgan Hill to wrap up the prune and walnut harvest. Then it was on to Los Angeles so Dad and Mother could take their second and last year of study in the Bible institute. We rented an apartment on Bonnie Brae Street, within walking distance of Angelus Temple.

From their youth, my parents had played musical instruments. Dad played the flute and piccolo; my mother, the piano and French horn. My brother, Donald, took up the trombone early in his life, and my sister, Barbara, studied the piano. My parents decided that the time had come for the youngest member of the family to begin on an instrument. Dad purchased a cornet, and I began taking lessons from a member of Angelus Temple who lived on the next block.

In those days, automobiles had running boards. Dad bought a collapsible pump organ, and many times during that school year, especially on Saturdays, the organ was strapped to the running board, and our entire family would travel in the car to wherever our parents had decided to hold a meeting, generally on the street and very often in a non-Caucasian neighborhood. My parents, who had already had a call to the mission field, felt that it was important to get as much experience as possible ministering to people of different cultures.

Dad and Mother also played their instruments in the Bible school band, and that meant playing, from time to time, in the services in the temple or in the branch churches pioneered and pastored by students from the Bible school. These churches held meetings in rented storefronts or in rented vacant churches; some were in building programs located in towns surrounding Los Angeles.

Our church home was Angelus Temple. We had become members during our first year in the city. It was our practice to attend several services each week, including all three services on Sundays.

One Sunday afternoon, during my folks' final semester of study, God told Dad to put all of his money in the offering. A few moments later, in the same service, Sister McPherson asked for testimonies. Dad briefly told how God had called him to be a missionary to Panama. We left the service, knowing that now the family purse was empty and bills would soon come. The next day, a letter came from a man whom my parents had, from time to time, helped financially. He wrote: "I know you don't need this, but I can't have any peace in my heart until I mail this check to you." The amount he sent, though not large, paid the bills until more funds came from the ranch. It was a lesson in trusting the Lord.

The next day, during the first session of the morning, came a request from Sister McPherson that my father come immediately to her office. She remembered his testimony from the afternoon before and asked him to tell in detail his missionary call. When he finished, she said, "Mr. Edwards, the Holy Spirit affirms to me that your call is of God. I now appoint you as a Foursquare missionary to Panama."

My parents graduated from the International Institute of Foursquare Evangelism on May 27, 1927. Two days later hands were laid on them as they were ordained for the ministry. Their certificate of ordination reads: "Be it known that Arthur and Edith Edwards were publicly set apart to the work of the Foursquare gospel...according to the usages of The Echo Park Evangelistic Association, Inc. of Los Angeles, California..." Their ordination papers were officially approved on January 1, 1928, and on the eighth of that month, during the annual Foursquare convention, my parents were licensed by the International Foursquare Gospel Lighthouses. Hands were laid on them as the entire convention body set them apart as missionaries to the Republic of Panama. They received new ordination certificates in May of that year.

My family sailed from Los Angeles Harbor on January 23, 1928, on the S.S. Manchuria bound for New York via the Panama Canal. Quite a large group from Angelus Temple came to the dock to see us off. As the gangplank was being removed and the ship started to sail, they sang: "God be with you 'til we meet again." Although the words of that hymn are very appropriate for such an occurrence, for me it is a song that has always meant separation from friends and loved ones. At the end of each furlough as we left to return to the mission field, I heard that same song. It seemed to remind everyone of the seriousness of missionary ministry—those staying behind to cover the missionaries with prayer and the ones departing—calling all to be faithful and do their best for the Lord.

All five of us stood at the railing on the deck of the ship's stern until the California coast dropped out of sight. Dad, Mother, Donald, Barbara, and I slept in bunk beds, and we shared a bathroom with other passengers. For the most part it was a good voyage; however, about the fifth day out, the crew began to tie down everything on deck. Soon all passengers were ordered inside and down below. Before long the waves were crashing over the ship, and we were in the midst of a very bad storm. We were in our stateroom praying for the storm to abate, when there was a knock at the door. Dad opened it and there stood a steward with a large platter of fresh fruit. He said that he heard the people singing the hymn as the ship got underway and finally had learned that we were a missionary family on our way to Panama. He was from a gospel church in New York and wanted to meet us. Dad asked him if the ship was going to make it. "This is a bad storm," he replied, "but God called you to Panama, and He is not going to allow the ship to sink. In fact, I feel safer with you aboard."

On the morning of February 1, 1928, the ship docked in Balboa Harbor, the Pacific entrance to the Panama Canal. After we went through immigration and customs, Mr. George Plankenhorn, the constable of the court in Balboa, met us. His family in Los Angeles had written to him that we would be sailing on the S. S. Manchuria. His wife had taken their four children to Los Angeles and rented a house near Angelus Temple. They asked neighbors where there was a good church to attend and were directed to the temple, where all of them found Christ. The oldest son, Luther, attended LIFE Bible College and pioneered the Goodyear Foursquare Church in Los Angeles (now known as the Florence Avenue Foursquare Church, in Santa Fe Springs, California). Aimee Semple McPherson often had him preach in the temple.

Mr. Plankenhorn took us from the boat to his quarters in Balboa, where we resided for the first few weeks. That first afternoon, all five of us walked from the Canal Zone into Panama City and sat down on benches in the Santa Ana Plaza, located in the heart of the city. As my parents watched the people, they were moved to tears of joy. The Holy Spirit once again witnessed to them that now they had arrived in the land of their calling.

Prior to our departure from Los Angeles, Dad had purchased a secondhand tent with its equipment—side poles and the tall center ones—and iron seat ends. Lumber for the bench seats and backs would be purchased locally in Panama. Along with our 1925 Studebaker car, these were shipped by freighter to the port of Balboa. The Foursquare Church was in its infancy, and a foreign missions department did not yet exist. When Dad and Mother were appointed as missionaries, they were promised that they would be sent to the field and supported financially. However, no specific monthly amount was agreed upon. They were eager to get to the field, and the Lord had supplied personal funds to ship the tent and car. Just before the boat pulled away from the dock, someone from the Angelus Temple office delivered a check for one hundred dollars to my folks. The Foursquare Church was very faithful in sending a monthly check from the time we arrived on the field.

The boat carrying the tent and car docked in Balboa Harbor. But it went on, crossing the canal and on to New York without unloading that cargo. Several weeks later, the ship returned, and the shipment was unloaded. It was well into the month of April before the tent and equipment were cleared through customs. A vacant lot was rented in Panama City in the section called Chorrillo.

Finally, the night had arrived for the opening of the Foursquare Gospel Crusade. The tent was up, electric lights had been installed, the benches made, and the platform erected. All five of us played our instruments: Dad, the flute; mother, the alto horn; Donald, the trombone; Barbara, the folding organ; and I, the cornet. We also sang special numbers together.

The tent could seat six hundred people and was packed to capacity. Everything started off well, but, after the first song, down came a hard tropical rain. In no time, the floor of the tent was covered with water, and people stood on top of the benches. The downpour continued, and before long almost everyone had gone. The beginning was not what we had anticipated.

In the midst of our disappointment someone said, "This rain is a sign from God that He is going to pour out showers of blessing upon Panama." From then on, one of the songs frequently used in the services was "Lluvias de Gracia" ("There Shall Be Showers of Blessing"). The tent meetings were short lived—the rainy season had come and the old secondhand tent could not withstand the hot sun and the heavy rains. Before long it was ripping apart. But souls had been saved, many people had been healed, and a group of new converts had become a reality.

After the tent had been taken down, my father rented an old frame church building in Guachapali, another section of the city. It was a church owned by a congregation of people from the West Indies who had come to Panama to work on the construction of the Panama Canal. They had their English-speaking services only on Sunday mornings, and, during the week, the building served as a day school for sons and daughters of the members. The Foursquare Church services were at night and, of course, in Spanish.

We rented another location near where the tent had stood. My mother became the pastor of that new work. Meetings were held at night. During the day, Dad and Mother often held street meetings and passed out tracts in different areas of the city. The Foursquare Church in Panama had become a reality.

At that time, my father was forty-seven years old, Mother was forty-four, Donald was sixteen, and Barbara was fifteen. I was the ripe old age of eight.

4

◁ A Vision Fulfilled

URING THE TIME that my father had attended the Bible institute in Los Angeles, he had often arisen early in the morning and walked to the school to spend time in prayer before classes began. In the spring of his final semester, while in prayer at the altar of the main classroom on the fourth floor of the school, God had given him a vision. In the vision, my father clearly saw an elderly man in a field with an old horse-drawn plow. The work had stopped, and this man with white hair and a white beard was leaning on the plow, with one hand to his brow. He was looking far off, as if watching for someone. The vision was very vivid, and, as Dad looked at the man, he could distinguish every feature of his face. The wind was lightly blowing his hair and beard. There was no message; no words were spoken. The vision faded, and the Lord gave no interpretation.

Unexpectedly one day, a few weeks after we arrived in Panama, my dad was called to the Gorgas Hospital in the Canal Zone, near Panama City. He was informed that an elderly missionary had been brought in from the interior of the country by a U. S. Army airplane. The hospital authorities requested that my father come and visit him. Upon entering the hospital room, my dad recognized the man lying on the bed. He was the man my father had seen in his vision! His eyes were closed, but he was talking in an unrecognizable language. A doctor and nurse were standing by the bed, and the doctor remarked, "I understand six languages, but this is not one of them. Do you know the language he is speaking?" Without further comment, they left the room, and Dad moved to the side of the bed where he could see more fully the face of this gentleman. The gentleman was speaking in other tongues, communing with his Lord. Soon thereafter, he passed away.

Mr. Latham, which we later learned was his name, was a veteran of the Spanish American War and a member of Cumberland Presbyterian Church. He had voluntarily gone to Panama to do missionary work in the interior of the country, supported by his limited military pension. He had settled in the town of Chitre, about 160 miles from Panama City, in an area where there was no gospel witness of any kind. There he had erected a one-room frame building for his home. His ministry had consisted of making friends with the people and passing out tracts. Although he left no established church work, he had become well known in that area and was called "El Tio" (the uncle) by those who knew him. His life was one of compassion and help for the people, and he was a man of prayer.

A few weeks following his death we made the trip to Chitre in our 1925 Studebaker touring car. We found Mr. Latham's little home and entered. On the wall was a framed picture of Aimee Semple McPherson, and on his table were several copies of her magazine, *The Bridal Call*. Dad found his diary and turned the pages to the time, about a year before, when my dad had seen the vision in Los Angeles, California. In the diary for that specific day, Mr. Latham had written: "I am now much along in years and my strength is waning. Lord, please span the miles and put your hand on someone else to come and take up the plow."

Sometimes new missionaries need confirmation of their place of service in the Lord's Harvest Field. The vision, the visit to the hospital room, seeing firsthand the man of the vision, and, a few weeks later, reading the entry in Mr. Latham's diary, did that for my parents.

To best understand the religious and social climate that existed in Panama at the time our family arrived, I divide the population of the country into four categories: 1.) Panamanians (Spanish-speaking); 2.) Immigrant laborers from the West Indies (mostly

English-speaking); 3.) U. S. employees of the Panama Canal, living in the Canal Zone; and 4.) Indian tribes.

Panamanians made up the major population of the country and most of them were Roman Catholic, in name if not by practice. Aside from the Catholic churches in virtually every city and town of any size, there were four Methodist churches in the entire country. All four congregations were small in number. For the Spanish-speaking population that was the church in Panama.

For the most part, immigrant workers were English-speaking men, and their families were from Jamaica and other islands of the West Indies in the Caribbean. They had been brought to Panama by the U. S. government to help in the construction of the Panama Canal; they had stayed on after the canal opened in 1914. A few hundred lived in the Canal Zone in government housing and were employed by the Canal, but the majority resided in Panama City and Colon, located on the Pacific and Atlantic coasts, respectively. They had brought their own religious ties with them: Anglican, Methodist, Baptist, Catholic, Salvation Army, and voodoo. These various groups were all non-Spanish speaking and relatively small in number.

The Canal Zone was an area leased from Panama, from coast to coast and five miles on each side of the canal channel. The majority of the residents in the Canal Zone were U. S. citizens since only those employed by the U. S. government could reside there. Each town had a Catholic church and a Union church, the latter to serve those not of the Catholic faith. On the Pacific side there was an Episcopal church, a Baptist church, and a Christian Science church. Repeated attempts by other denominations to start church services in the Canal Zone were unsuccessful because they were denied permits from the Canal government. Applicants were told that there were already a sufficient number of churches.

Three main Indian tribes inhabited the Republic of Panama. The Choco lived in the southeast area near the border with

Colombia, on the Pacific side. The Kuna (San Blas) could be found along the north coast (Atlantic) near Colombia. The Guaymi resided in the mountain areas of the Chiriquí and Bocas del Toro provinces near the border with Costa Rica. There were no churches, and the nearest thing to religion was witchcraft. The witchdoctor had much power in the tribe.

As far as we could tell when we arrived, there was no group or gathering of Pentecostal believers in any part of the country. Within the Spanish-speaking population, only four small Protestant congregations could be identified. The church in the Canal Zone had its vision pointed inward; there was no activity to reach those on the outside. The church with the West Indies people kept within its own culture and language group.

My parents were definitely led by God to the Spanish-speaking people. Their vision was for the whole country. The Acts of the Apostles was their "Manual of Operation." As students in the Bible institute, they had studied the Book of Acts under the teaching of Aimee Semple McPherson. Through the first months in Panama, Dad prayerfully studied that book again and again. In those days, missionary books telling how to minister in foreign lands were almost nonexistent. Dad and Mother were very dependent upon Scripture and the direction of the Holy Spirit. Both of them spent much time in prayer, seeking the leading of the Lord. Prior to their appointment as missionaries, their practical ministerial experience had consisted of pioneering three churches in California and street ministry during their Bible college days. Now they were confronted with a very needy field, and their hearts were full of compassion and love for the Panamanian people.

5

◁ With Signs Following

I T WAS A Sunday morning in July 1928. Our family got up early and drove to Gamboa, Canal Zone, a distance of about twenty miles, to take the train to Frijoles, a little town on the Panama Railroad. A stranger had invited my dad to come to Frijoles, along with his family, to conduct a religious service. The only means of transportation from Panama City to Colon, the two terminal Panamanian cities of the Canal, was by the Panama Railroad. Frijoles was the midpoint.

We got off of the train and carried our instruments, a large roll of several sheets of heavy craft paper, and the wooden stand on which to hang it. On each five-by-four-foot sheet Dad had used a small paintbrush to write in Spanish the words of well-known hymns. He always said, "Get the people to sing songs that teach the gospel and soon they will be singing the gospel as they go about their everyday lives."

We set up our equipment under the shade of a large mango tree in the center of the small town and started playing our instruments. Soon, the people had gathered. They came from everywhere, and Dad had them singing some of the songs. He turned to another sheet he had painted, showing two roads. There was a wide road, curving downward like a snake, leading to hell. The narrow one went straight and upwards into heaven. At the intersection of the roads there was a cross.

Dad preached Jesus, the One who is the Way to heaven and eternal life. In his message he mentioned that God also heals. At the conclusion of his message, he made a call for people to give their hearts to the Lord. No one responded except a young man. Rosendo de Orta, twenty-years-old, came forward out of the crowd. He pulled up one pant leg above his knee and revealed a terribly infected sore that extended from just above the ankle almost to his knee. It was very ugly and was damp with pus pockets. He had been to a medical doctor and a witchdoctor but to no avail; gangrene poisoning had set in. Pointing to the wound he said, "You say you can heal! Heal that!" Dad calmly replied, "I don't heal, but my God does. If you want us to, we will ask Jesus to heal you." Of course, Rosendo consented. My dad prayed a short prayer, loud enough for all to hear. The people were informed that we would be back under that tree in the early afternoon for another gathering. We retreated to the shade of another tree a short distance away and ate our lunch.

That afternoon we had hardly finished singing the first song, when this same young man returned to the front and pulled up his pant leg. That terrible, huge sore had dried up, and people said a miracle had taken place. Rosendo brought his brother, Santos, who asked for prayer for his stomach trouble. God healed him immediately. At the end of the meeting, those two young men said, "If you will return here next Sunday, we will go from home to home over this entire area and tell the people what we have seen and heard."

During the days that followed, the news of what had happened that Sunday in Frijoles spread far and wide. The next Sunday we again went to Frijoles. That was the beginning of Sunday services in Frijoles for many months to follow. What God did in that place could easily be a book in itself. People began coming from other areas. Trains brought people from Panama City and Colon. They had heard that God was doing things in Frijoles. The Panama Railroad soon had to put extra coaches on the trains to Frijoles each Sunday. People gave their hearts to the Lord, and God did many miracles, healing sick bodies of many kinds of afflictions and diseases.

One Sunday a mother brought her eight-year-old son forward for prayer. The lad was dumb and had never spoken a word in his life. My mother prayed for him and then said, "Diga 'Jesús,'"

("Say, 'Jesus'"). After just a couple of efforts, he audibly pronounced the name, clear and strong. Then Mother said, "Diga 'Mamá,'" ("Say, 'Mother'"). I shall never forget seeing the tears of joy that streamed down the mother's face when her little son said, "Mamá," for the first time in his life. They came each week to the services, and in no time the little guy was speaking like any normal child his age.

In the Bible, the phrase *signs and wonders* refers to God's intervention in the natural affairs of His creation. The term *signs* refers to what God does, and the word *wonders* records the response of the people. That was the way the Foursquare Church in Panama grew. Signs and wonders brought the people to see what God was doing. When they saw the work of God in action, they believed.

In the Book of Acts, when Philip went to Samaria, the people saw and heard the message of Jesus. And in 1 John 1, we hear the testimony of "the disciple whom Jesus loved." He writes: "That...which we have heard, which we have seen with our eyes, which we have looked upon, and our hands have handled.... declare we unto you" (1 John 1:1, 3, KJV).

6

◁ Pentecost in Frijoles

EVERY SUNDAY OUR family, all five of us, took the train to the town of Frijoles. We conducted morning and after-noon services and then returned on the train to Panama City for the evening service. Dad and Mother were a strong ministry team. Dad was gifted in evangelism, and Mother had a strong teaching ministry. Almost every Sunday morning there would be new people receiving the Lord as Savior.

The next event of the day was the water baptismal service. This occurred during the two-hour break between services, which were held under the large tree in the center of the village. Just down the hill was an inlet of the Gatun Lake which made a perfect baptistery.

My parents believed that the New Testament example was water baptism as soon as possible after conversion, even the same day. Believers and nonbelievers alike would line the bank of the lake to witness the event. Before immersion, each convert would give a personal testimony of receiving Jesus as Savior. Frequently, as they listened to the testimonies, nonbelievers on the bank would find Christ.

The afternoon service was mostly a teaching time, given to doctrine and Christian living. Trains from Panama City and Colon, cities at the Pacific and Atlantic entrances to the Panama Canal, brought more people seeking the gospel. Men and women were accepting Jesus as their Savior, and God continued to heal the sick.

At the entrance of Frijoles, across the tracks, lived the section boss of the Panama Railroad. His large, one-story house was built upon ten-foot posts over a concrete floor. This man came to my dad and said, "I want to offer you, free of charge, the open air basement of my house in which to hold your religious services each Sunday. The rainy season has set in, and you have been lucky that none of your meetings have been rained out. Since you have come to this place, we haven't had to call the police to stop fights and crime." We held church services there for several months.

A very capable and newly converted lady became my parents' interpreter. She had a great desire to learn God's Word and to serve Him. One particular Sunday morning on the train, she said to my folks, "There is something that I want to receive more than anything else in all the world. I want to receive the baptism of the Holy Spirit. But I hear that my whole body would tremble and shake and fall on the floor. I am afraid." My parents replied, "You don't have to have that happen. God loves you and desires to fill you with His Spirit even more than you want to receive Him."

Soon after the service began, Dad called on his interpreter to lead in prayer. She started praying in Spanish, and suddenly she was speaking in a tongue she did not know, "as the Spirit gave them utterance" (Acts 2:4). This very young congregation had not yet been taught about the baptism with the Holy Spirit. But when the people heard this lady speak in tongues and sensed a supernatural presence of the Lord, everyone voluntarily knelt down and began to speak to God out of their hearts. Everyone was praying audibly. It was as if an invisible cloud of God's glory hovered over that place. Soon there were others who began to speak in tongues. Nothing was out of order. It was like a united body of people, filled with God's love, lifting their voices in chorus to Him. Prayer continued unabated for at least an hour. No one wanted to leave.

At the conclusion of the service, Rosendo de Orta came to Dad and Mother, unfolding a piece of paper that he had just taken out of his shirt pocket. He was the young man who had been healed in the first service held in that town. He said, "I was waiting for an opportunity to read this aloud to all in attendance, but what has just happened proves that the message of this letter is false. I, too, have just received this wonderful infilling of the Holy Spirit with the speaking in tongues."

Prior to this, Dad and Mother had started their ministry without giving much time to learning the Spanish language. From the start there were those who volunteered to interpret. The most efficient one was a lawyer in Panama City who had come to know the Lord and was eager to serve in that capacity, especially on each Sunday in the Frijoles meetings. The rapid growth in attendance at those services, however, caused the lawyer to become proud, and Dad had to dismiss him and enlist someone else. The letter that Rosendo brought had been written by this former interpreter for my parents. Being a lawyer, he had very skillfully written a letter declaring that the speaking in other tongues today was of the devil. The letter stated that speaking in other tongues ended with the apostles' era. Well, God had beaten the devil to the punch!

Those who had received that experience that day began to spread the message of the grace of God with great boldness. Some suffered severe persecution but spoke the gospel with authority and love. There were those who were concerned about their loved ones in ill health and went to them with the message of Jesus, the Great Physician. God answered their prayers, and many were healed miraculously.

Within a short time, these newly baptized saints of God were conducting home prayer meetings with the reading of the Word. Foursquare churches were soon started in Colon, Chilibre, Caño Quebrado, and Limón. At the same time, many more people were being added to the church in Panama City. Several of those who later would become leading Foursquare ministers were saved, baptized in water, and filled with the Spirit in Frijoles. There is no way of knowing just how far the results of that day carried. Over the years, I have met people from the Frijoles meetings in many parts of Panama and in a few other countries.

The experience that day was a turning point. The Foursquare Church in Panama was "off and running."

Dad saw in the Acts of the Apostles how Paul started churches in centers of education, commerce, and civilization. The apostles led to the Lord people who had the ability to take the gospel to those cities and surrounding provinces and countries. Going to Frijoles had not been planned. It was just a small village in the center of a rural area of small farms tilled by country people. But the outpouring of the Spirit of God brought people from the two main cities of the country, people of much ability. Upon giving their hearts to Christ, being filled with His Spirit, and receiving teaching from the Word of God, they began taking the message to others.

Over a year had gone by since the first service had been held in the little town of Frijoles. The section boss of the Panama Railroad had been very kind in allowing the Sunday morning and afternoon services to be held in the open-air basement of his house. But the congregation kept growing. More and more people were being saved, healed, baptized with the Holy Spirit, and growing in the Lord.

About ten miles north on the railroad at Monte Lirio, the next station, were two buildings that were no longer being used. Each building contained four apartments, two stories high, and built of wood with corrugated iron roofs. They had been built and used during the construction of the Panama Canal, and they were to be sold to the highest bidder. Dad's bid of twenty dollars got the structures, and men from Frijoles worked with him in the demolition. It cost the same amount to rent two railroad flat cars, loaded with the secondhand lumber and roofing. A locomotive pulled them to Frijoles, where the men unloaded the material. During the next several days, Dad and my seventeen-year-old brother, Donald, worked with these men who were all new in the faith. The first Foursquare church in Panama was built on a lot leased for one dollar a year from the Panama Canal Company. It was built for the tropical weather, with an open space under the corrugated iron roof around all four sides, and many windows. The building, with its wooden floor, rested on posts a few feet above the ground.

In the beginning years of the Foursquare Church movement, church buildings were often called "lighthouses." Some of the churches in Southern California erected lighthouses above their front entrances. To enter the sanctuary of the church in South Gate, a suburb of Los Angeles, you walked through the door of a large lighthouse. In the front of this new church in Frijoles, Dad painted a lighthouse with the name *Jesus* on the light chamber and with four beams of light. One had the word *Savior*, another the word *Healer*, a third, *Baptizer*, and the last, *Coming King*. Of course, these words were written in Spanish.

After the outpouring of the Holy Spirit in Frijoles, several of those who had received the baptism with the Holy Spirit took the Foursquare gospel to relatives living in other areas. Home meetings began in several places, and it was not long before some of these became established congregations. God raised up leaders who, although new in the faith, were the early national pastors. They came to my parents frequently for Bible studies and encouragement. I think the best explanation is that there was a spontaneous move of the Holy Spirit upon their lives.

Attending Angelus Temple from 1925 to 1928, our family learned a chorus that was always sung in a loud and bombastic style. It contained only two words: *alleluia* and *amen*. It became one of the most popular worship songs in those years. After our arrival in Panama, Dad made his large charts containing the words of hymns and choruses in Spanish for use indoors and outdoors. That chorus did not have to be translated from English into Spanish, for those words are the same in both languages. We sang it so often that it began to be associated with our family.

We became well known in outlying villages. Often, as we were driving into town where an open-air service would be held, the people along the street would shout, "Llegaron los Aleluyas" ("The Alleluias have arrived"). By the time we had unpacked our instruments, set up the organ and the song charts, a crowd would have gathered, even before the first note was sung.

Many people accepted Jesus as their Savior in those meetings. People were invited to come forward and accept Jesus as Savior, and in addition, prayer was offered for those who were sick, and many were healed. As time went by and as the work spread from place to place, several of those converts became leaders in the ministry. Often, my parents took two or three of these new Christians with them to the open-air services. They were encouraged to take part by giving testimony of what God had done for them, leading the singing, or in preaching. When Dad and Mother preached, they preached the Word, always giving a positive message that was filled with the love of God and the offering of new life in Christ to anyone who would believe on His Name. They taught their workers to do the same. They were not to speak out against other religions but were to lift up Christ.

A large crowd gathered in the open-air service held in the village of Chepo. The song service had gone well, and Dad was into his message when, all of a sudden, a hush came over the entire crowd. Looking up the street, we saw the village religious leader coming, accompanied by a small gang of young men. As they drew near, the leader called for a demonstration against the "Aleluyas." The young men began throwing stones at us as well as at the national workers who were helping. Suddenly, Rosendo de Orta stood up by the song chart and, pointing his hand at the group, began speaking in tongues in a loud voice. All rock throwing immediately ceased, and everyone stood in rapt attention. When Rosendo finished his message in tongues, the man called off his gang and left, hurrying back up the street. The crowd stayed, Dad continued the message, and the service was concluded in the normal manner. Rosendo was healed in the meetings in Frijoles in July 1928, and he had continued to serve the Lord faithfully and attend services.

The next week when we returned to Chepo for another service, people told us what had happened the day following the service of the week before. The leader had called in several of the villagers and said to them, "That man [Rosendo] spoke in Latin, and I understood every word. He talked about Jesus Christ. What those Aleluyas are preaching is the truth." Within a few days that man had been dismissed from his work.

A few months later, in Capira, the religious authority in that town interrupted the open-air service, trying to stop the meeting. However, the crowd in attendance gave him no heed. He withdrew a short distance and listened to the message that was being delivered by one of the national workers. After the service was over, Dad took the two national workers who were with him and called on the priest in his residence. He was cordial and invited them to enter. He then started the conversation by saying that he was the only authorized representative of God in that area. In the conversation that followed, he was asked how many of the residents of that place were real followers of the Lord. He replied, "None." Dad said, "Then you need our help to lead them to Christ." To this he replied, "Yes, I really need help." He too was dismissed from his position.

As the work grew, we needed printed words of the hymns and choruses we sang. Dad had his song charts, and often the people would copy the words, writing them in notebooks. The songs taught Bible doctrine as well as offering words of praise to the Lord. The handmade benches in the facilities being used for church services were not made with racks in which to place hymnals. Orders were sent to a publishing house in Texas that printed hymnbooks in Spanish, *Himnos de Gloria*. Some hymnals contained only the lyrics; others included the musical scores. The latter were more expensive. It was not long before almost every family in the Foursquare congregations across the land had a songbook.

They purchased the hymnals as well as their Bibles. We found that, when the hymnal and the Bible were kept together, the people read their Bibles daily and also sang songs out of the hymnal in their daily devotions at home. As a teenager growing up in Panama and taking part in the services, I was very impressed to see almost all the people raise their Bibles above their heads when the leader of the service asked how many had brought their Bibles.

The village of Chepo was at the end of the road going toward Colombia. Many were saved there, and soon a church building was constructed from secondhand building materials. From time to time there were buildings in the Canal Zone that were no longer needed and were put up for bid. Generally, Dad's bid was successful. Some of the new believers would help him tear down the buildings and move the material to where the church would be built.

In a rural area called Chivo Chivo lived many people who had come from the West Indies and were English-speaking. They requested that my parents hold services in their area. As a result, two congregations developed. They used secondhand lumber and corrugated iron roofing from the Canal Zone to construct two small church buildings.

There were several other towns where we held meetings. Just prior to our arrival in Panama, a two-lane highway had been built in the interior of the country, west from Panama City as far as Santiago and Chitre, some 160 miles. To go into the interior, it was necessary to cross the canal by ferry at the Pedro Miguel Locks.

One of the towns where we held meetings was Chame. We stayed there for several days, holding meetings at night and canvassing the town each day and handing out tracts. A few days later, back home, all five of us came down with malaria. I was admitted to the Gorgas Hospital in the Canal Zone, and the doctors did not expect me to live through the night. Mother received permission to stay with me in the hospital room. Dad sent a cable to the prayer tower in Angelus Temple, asking for prayer for all of us. After six days, I was allowed to go home, but I had to take quinine, the liquid kind, for a long time afterward. Time and again I would come home from school with a burning fever.

But while I was still in the hospital, something unusual happened at home. One night after Dad had retired with fever and chills, the devil came into the room and sat on the foot of his bed and laughed at him, saying, "Here you are, Edwards, in Panama preaching that Jesus Christ is the same today as in yesteryear and that He is the Healer. Look at yourself." Dad raised up in bed and said, "Old Devil, in Jesus' name, I am going to knock you for a loop!" He was immediately healed of the malaria, and God blessed him in the healing ministry.

Over the years that followed, I often worked with him in services. Many people came with malaria fever, asking for prayer. I cannot remember a single person who was not healed immediately from the fever. Dad would put his hand on their foreheads and pray in the name of Jesus, as the Scripture instructs in Mark 16:18: "They will lay their hands on the sick, and they will recover."

7

◁ Taking the Gospel to the Darien Province

THE ISTHMUS OF Panama has a very extensive history, relating to several Indian tribes and their cultures. As in the other areas of the Americas, Indian civilizations rose and fell. When the Spanish came to what is now Panama, the tribal people resisted them and, at times, inflicted heavy losses on Spanish soldiers. In time peace was made, and today there are three tribes. The Kuna, known generally as the San Blas, live on the islands along the coast of northeast Panama. The Guaymí inhabit the mountains of the west toward Costa Rica. The Choco live on the banks of the rivers in the Darien Province, bordering Colombia. The Foursquare Church has congregations in all three tribes. The first ones touched by the gospel were from the Choco, on the banks of the Chucunaque River in the Darien Province.

One Sunday morning in Frijoles my mother preached on the Second Coming of Jesus Christ. A young man named Harmodio gave his heart to the Lord and was baptized in water. In the afternoon service, he received the infilling of the Holy Spirit with the evidence of speaking in tongues. He purchased a Bible that was small enough to fit in his shirt pocket and came each Sunday for about six weeks. Then several weeks went by without Harmodio in the services. One Monday morning there was a knock at the door of our residence in Panama City. There stood Harmodio, saying he had a big problem. After being invited to enter and to take a seat, he told his story.

Harmodio had gone from Frijoles to work on the other side of Gatun Lake, cutting bananas. During the lunch break he would read his little New Testament. His fellow laborers wanted to know what he was reading and began to ask questions. He finally told them that he would tell them about the book if they would come together on Sunday morning in the nearby small village of Caño Quebrado.

"That was yesterday," he said. "I decided to hold a service and started about ten o' clock, singing all of the songs and choruses I had learned. Then I preached to them all I had heard in the messages in Frijoles. Finally, at four o'clock, I did what you do. I gave a call for others to receive Jesus as Savior. Forty men came forward and accepted the Lord. Now here is my big problem: what do I do with them?" My parents gave a very wise answer: "God has given you these people. We will teach you, and you will teach them."

God blessed Harmodio, and the young church grew rapidly. Whole families came to Christ, to the extent that the entire village came to know the Savior. The new believers then built a church building. Harmodio was a very successful and dedicated pastor to them. Then one day he announced that he would soon be making a long journey. He wanted to return to where his father lived on the Atrato River in Colombia to give him the Good News.

"He has never heard the gospel, and I must take it to him." His mother had left his father when Harmodio was a small child, moving to Panama. Now, Harmodio was to become the first national missionary of the Panama Foursquare Church.

Harmodio made the trip on a small coastal vessel that traveled from Panama City, southeast down the coast to the Tuira River in the Darien. Going inland on that river he noticed villages along the banks. Finally, at the town of El Real about sixty miles inland, the boat had gone as far as the river was navigable. From there Harmodio would have to travel by foot through the dense jungles of the Darien, on trails unknown to him, and across the border to where his father lived and where he had been born.

While in El Real, he decided to hold a service, preaching the gospel to a people who had never heard the message of salvation. He started walking toward his destination and came to another village and again held a service. After the meeting was over, a man came to him and said, "You are Harmodio Palacio. I am your brother. I have come from our father's home and tomorrow I start the return trip and you can go with me, for I know the way." Meeting with his brother was not coincidental, but a divine intervention.

After several days and nights on the trail, they arrived at their destination. Harmodio led his father to the Lord and started three churches in that far western section of Colombia, far from the "outside world."

Returning to Panama, Harmodio resumed his ministry in the Caño Quebrado Church. He would often come to our home and spend hours at a time with my parents in Bible study and prayer. One day I gave to Harmodio my cornet, which I had played since I was eight, and taught him to play it. Although I had played it in services from the start of my parents' ministry in Panama, I knew that a musical instrument would be a tremendous addition to Harmodio's services. Soon afterward our furlough came, and I purchased a trumpet at a pawnshop on Main Street in Los Angeles.

Time passed. One day Harmodio said that when he made that trip to Colombia, he saw village after village along the rivers of the Darien and knew they had never heard the gospel. He felt the call of God to go to them. On that trip, in six weeks' time in those riverbank villages, he led more than one thousand, six hundred people to Christ. It was not long before he moved to Yaviza, a small village on the banks of the Chucunaque River. The people of Yaviza did business with the Choco Indian tribe. God blessed Harmodio's ministry in Yaviza, a church was started, and the new converts built a church of reed sides and corrugated iron roof. His congregation was composed mostly of Spanish-speaking men and women, most of them descendants of slaves, like himself, from Colombia.

The Choco Indians lived out from these trading post villages, along the banks of the rivers. The typical Choco house had a floor of tree bark and sat about six feet above the ground on logs with a thatch roof above and no sides. The floor is accessible by a notched log that even their dogs learn to run up and down on. At night the log is pulled up when the family is "inside." Choco men wear a loincloth, and the women a wraparound covering from their hips down to about the knees. They speak the Choco language, which was not transliterated until several years later by our missionaries.

Most of the Chocos had small farms on which they raised plantains. The plantain looks like a banana, but is larger and a common staple in the diet of people of all classes in tropical America. It is not eaten raw, but cooked, and is rich in iron.

There were no roads in the Darien. All travel was by boats on the rivers. The Chocos made their boats by hollowing out logs and shaping them into a type of a flat bottom canoe called a piragua. Most piraguas have a four-foot beam and are twenty to thirty feet long. These canoes could carry quite a load as they are poled up and down the rivers. The Chocos used them to get their crops to market. Plantains grow the year around and, when the Choco has enough to fill his piragua, he goes downstream to the village and sells the load to a buyer, generally an employee of the town saloon. He is usually paid by credit at the local trading post, including cheap liquor.

The "religion" of the Indian is witchcraft and consists mainly of appeasing the spirits. It is a practice of putting curses on people, on planting and preventing harvest, and the lifting of those curses—all done by the witchdoctor. Although the Choco comes into the village and sometimes even as far as Panama City, he keeps mostly to himself. The Chocos very seldom mix with other races. They do not live in villages, but in huts scattered along the riverbanks. Because they loved seclusion, the Chocos would not enter the church. They stayed outside, listening and looking through the open windows and door.

One day there was a knock at the door of Harmodio's residence at the back of the church. There stood Faustino Pacheco, affectionately called by everyone "Chicheme," a Choco man dressed in only his loincloth. He said that he was sick, that he could not stay away from liquor, and that when he drank he would cough up blood. He had seen that the God of Harmodio could heal and cure people from craving aguardiente, or firewater. The pastor invited him into the church to tell him about Jesus. Around the church interior walls were full-color pictures depicting the life of Christ. Harmodio tried his best to explain Jesus to him. But this message was very different from what Chicheme was accustomed to. How could a god allow his son to become a sacrifice? When it seemed hopeless, Harmodio opened his Bible and put it against the naked chest of Chicheme. He asked God to do what is impossible for man to do, to reveal Jesus Christ to this Choco and heal him, too.

Bright and early the next morning, there was another knock at the door. There stood the same man, but this time with his piragua paddle in hand. He said, "I have come for you to loan me that book. I am now well. I do not desire to drink anymore. I left my woman, the mother of my children, very sick. We live up the river far from here. Loan me the book, so I can make her well." The pastor did his best to explain to Chicheme that the book was in Spanish and it would not help because he would not be able to read it, that it was made of paper and ink and not an idol to be worshiped. Finally, the only way to "get rid" of Chicheme was to loan him the Bible.

All day long the book went up the river in the piragua poled by this Choco man. He reached his home and tied up his boat at the bank, took the book and climbed up the notched log into his house. He told his mate what had happened to him and how he had been made well. He opened the book and put it on her chest and made his prayer to his newfound Lord. Only God in heaven knows what he said in that prayer. But God understands the heart, and He answered Chicheme's petition, healing that woman and raising her up. A few days later Chicheme returned to Yaviza and gave the book back to its owner. God had healed and also saved two Chocos. This marked the beginning of a ministry that would reach large numbers of Chocos.

Soon after, I made a trip to Yaviza. I met Chicheme and his family. What a joy it was to have the fellowship with my new brother and sister in the Lord. On the wall of our home is a framed picture of this family on the bank of the Chucunaque River.

In the Darien, the usual way to bathe is in the nearby river. On one of my trips, Harmodio and I got our baths by swimming in the Chucunaque River. I noticed calluses on Harmodio's knees. When I asked about them, he replied that they were the result of spending time in prayer.

It is not possible to talk about the Darien without mentioning Vinton and Verna Johnson, who came to Panama in 1949. Vinton was an accomplished linguist both in biblical languages and Spanish, a skill that would allow him to accurately bridge the gap between what would become their written language and the Scriptures. After working with us in the Bible institute, the Johnsons were assigned to lead the Foursquare Church in the Chiriquí Province. With the increase in the converts of the Choco tribe in the Darien, we decided that the time had come for missionaries to go to the village of Yaviza and work with the people. The Choco dialect had never been written, so Vinton began to learn Choco, with the intent of reducing it to writing so that they might eventually have the Scriptures in their own language.

Because of a larger concentration of Chocos in the Sambu area of the province, it was decided that Vinton and Verna should relocate. However, there was no building in Sambu available for their residence. Ernesto Murillo, one of our national pastors from Panama City was sent to Sambu to build the living quarters from cement block. Included in the construction would be a full open-air basement, which would become the meeting place for the new church. In addition to being a pastor, Ernesto was a building contractor. He worked on the building during the day; at night, he held meetings for the Chocos in the area.

Prior to this time, a Norwegian naturalist had spent a month in the Darien studying the Choco tribe. He returned home and wrote a book about them. In his book, he mentioned Bigua, the witchdoctor. He had told Bigua that he had traveled all over the world and had made friends with a lot of people in different places. One day, Bigua asked the naturalist if he knew there was a "principal god." The naturalist replied that he didn't know if there was such a god, or who he might be. Bigua observed, "You have traveled so far and still do not know?" Little did Bigua realize that he would soon find the answer to his own question.

The number of Chocos receiving Christ as Savior increased, with several being healed in the meetings. Hearing of the miracles of healing, Bigua, the main witchdoctor of the entire tribe, traveled several miles to Sambu to see who the "super witchdoctor" was. It was not long before Bigua recognized that there was a Healer much greater than himself. He gave his heart to Jesus, renounced witchcraft, and became a true follower of the Lord.

There are people of all races, cultures—whether civilized or not—who in their hearts are searching for the truth about God. What a privilege it was to be able to see the beginning of God's work in a group of people who had never before heard of Him.

8

◁ Our First Missionary Term and Furlough

MY FAMILY'S FIRST three years in Panama were hard ones, but God had blessed our ministry. The sudden crash of the stock market in 1929 triggered a worldwide economic depression. However, the missionary-sending church in the United States, Angelus Temple, together with its branch churches, had been faithful in sending their monthly support. Funds from the prune and walnut ranch in California, though meager, helped meet extra expenses in the work.

At least five church buildings made of secondhand lumber and roofing were erected in rural areas. The church in Panama City met in rented facilities; home meetings were being conducted regularly in several areas. The Foursquare Church in the Republic of Panama now consisted of several organized congregations.

At the time Dad and Mother were appointed Foursquare missionaries to Panama, they were asked how long they planned to stay in that country. Dad replied, "Three years."

In 1930 the entire family came down with malaria–fever and chills. All of us, except Dad, took quinine during the following months. I would often come home from school with malaria fever. Mother had become quite frail, and the whole family needed a good rest. In May 1931, a furlough was approved and it was decided that Mother, Barbara, and I would go first. Dad and Donald stayed behind until a supply missionary unit was sent to Panama to minister during our absence.

After the three of us had left for California, there was a very unusual happening one night in the house in Panama. Dad was suddenly awakened and, in the darkness, saw a man crouched at the foot of his bed. Dad sat up in bed, pointed his hand at the intruder, and began to speak in tongues in a loud voice. The would-be-robber became totally paralyzed. Dad told Donald to get up and turn on the light. Still, the man could not move from his crouched position. Finally, when Dad commanded him to get out, he was able to move and left. From then on, Dad always claimed that the gift of tongues was a powerful weapon. That incident was also another powerful sign that the Lord was blessing my parents' ministry in Panama.

A few days after our arrival in Los Angeles, Mother met Frank and Juventina Moncivaiz. They had graduated from LIFE Bible College in 1930 and were assisting in the McPherson Mexican Mission Church, El Buen Pastor, in Boyle Heights, Los Angeles. They were soon appointed as Foursquare missionaries and sailed down the west coast to Panama in September 1931. After a short orientation, they assumed the leadership of the Panama Field so that Dad and Donald could go on furlough.

Our whole family was together again, on our first furlough in Los Angeles. We lived in a rented apartment near Angelus Temple and spoke in Foursquare churches throughout the area. Dad went to an automobile auction and, with the high bid of seventy-five dollars, became the proud owner of a four-door Chrysler. I do not remember how old it was, but it had one major problem. It heated up, and frequent stops had to be made at service stations to put water in the radiator. Twice Dad and student friends from LIFE worked on it, taking off the radiator, cleaning out the whole system, but it still boiled.

This was also the first missionary furlough for the young Foursquare missions department. What the furloughing missionary did was mostly of his own initiative. Dad wanted to get out to the churches in other states and tell them what God had done in Panama and how their missionary offerings were bearing much fruit on foreign soil. Believing that the Chrysler was duly repaired, Dad, Mother, Donald, and I set out, going east for meetings every night in a different church. It was to be a trip of several weeks that would take us as far north as Minneapolis, Minnesota. My sister, Barbara, remained in Los Angeles to plan for her forthcoming wedding.

Before we had gotten to Pasadena, twelve miles to the east, the car was boiled over again. Dad drove into a used car lot on Colorado Boulevard and traded the car in for another vehicle, this time a Jewett sedan. The owner of the lot accepted the Chrysler as down payment and let us take this other vehicle on small monthly payments. We loaded our suitcases and equipment into the Jewett, and within a few minutes we were on our way.

The Great Depression hit the economy hard, but the small offerings we received in the missionary meetings paid for the gasoline and travel expenses. At each church the pastors divided us into two parties for the night. Dad and Mother generally stayed in the home of the pastors, Donald and I in the home of members of the local church. Souls were saved in the meetings, and people were stirred up for the Foursquare missionary ministry worldwide.

While in Minnesota we took a couple of days off to visit my father's hometown, Spring Valley. We got to meet a lot of people that Dad knew when he was a youth before he migrated to California in the early part of the 1900s. We also enjoyed being with family in Morgan Hill, California. In fact, it was in Morgan Hill that we enjoyed a Christmas family reunion.

The 1932 annual convention of the Foursquare Church took place at Angelus Temple during the first ten days of January. The services were a blessing and inspiration for us all. My parents had a good time of fellowship with men and women who were students in LIFE Bible College from 1925 to 1927. They also met and made friends with others who were now ministering in various parts of the United States. One of their pastor friends was in need of a car but had no money, so Dad gave him the Jewett. There were only two small monthly payments left. The new owner accepted the offer with great joy and thanksgiving.

One afternoon in a home wedding, my sister Barbara was

married to Benjamin Rebmann, a student in LIFE Bible College and from Zion, Illinois. Dad performed the marriage.

When the convention was over, we were soon out on the high seas en route down the west coast on our return to Panama. But there were now just three of the Edwards clan. Barbara now lived in Los Angeles with her husband, and Donald was enrolled as a student in LIFE Bible College. He returned to Panama after graduation to continue his ministry.

9

◁ Expanding the Work

FRANK AND JUVENTINA Moncivaiz, with their infant son, Daniel, arrived in Panama in September of 1931 as supply missionaries while our family was on furlough. Both Frank and Juventina were ordained ministers of the Foursquare Church. They pastored the church in Panama City and traveled by train each Sunday morning to minister in the church at Frijoles.

In January 1932, Dad, Mother, and I returned to Panama from furlough. At that time, we shared a home with the Moncivaiz family in Panama City. A second church was started in another section of the capital in a rented hall on a corner building with three sets of double doors. Two of the sets of double doors opened onto the sidewalk of a busy street, which was one of the main routes of city buses. For the most part, "buses" were privately owned and were called chivas, or "nanny goats." They were constructed locally on the chassis of small truck bodies and painted many different bright colors. They were assigned to different routes within the city and outlying areas.

Services were held every night in the second church, with Sunday school and morning worship on Sunday morning. It was a pioneer endeavor, but within a few months the congregation filled the hall. Most of the people had been saved in the meetings we held there. At night, the place was packed full, and the doorways were filled with people out on the sidewalk, listening to the service.

At the first church, meetings were conducted on Sunday, Wednesday, and Friday nights—with Friday nights for the youth. The two congregations were growing, and the missionaries were teaching those whom God was raising up to be workers, giving them opportunities to lead the singing and to preach. They were gaining experience in leadership, with open doors to minister in outlying towns: Arraijan, Chorrera, Juan Diaz, Pueblo Nuevo, Pacora, and Chepo to name a few.

Early in the 1930s, Dad had the foresight to officially register the International Church of the Foursquare Gospel with the Panamanian government. The international bylaws and the articles of faith were the core of this legal document, and my dad held the power of attorney. The national government thereby granted the legal right to the Foursquare Church to carry out its ministry within the nation and to acquire and own property. During the ensuing years there were many times when local authorities, opposed to the gospel, tried to close the door to the Foursquare Church, but the law required them to back off. The Foursquare Church had been granted the right to exercise the ministry anywhere within the national boundaries.

In mid-1932, the United States government built a two-lane concrete road from Summit, Canal Zone, which passed through Chilibre, to the Chagres River. Construction was started on a large dam that, when completed, created a large lake to serve as a reservoir for the water used in the operation of the Panama Canal. People migrated to the area, mainly for agricultural purposes. Some moved from Frijoles, taking the gospel with them. Another Foursquare church was established in that area. Pioneer services had started in Colon and Limon on the Atlantic side of the isthmus.

With the spread of the work from the Pacific to the Atlantic, my family moved to Gamboa, in the Canal Zone. Gamboa was about halfway across the isthmus and at the end of the highway from Panama City. The Panama Railroad operated from coast to coast, paralleling the Panama Canal, with four passenger trains daily between Panama City and Colon. Living in Gamboa, we were in the geographical center of the established Foursquare churches.

At the same time, my brother, Donald, returned to Panama after graduating from LIFE Bible College in Los Angeles. He became involved immediately in the ministry. Our family now had three Foursquare ministers working in the country, often holding meetings simultaneously in different areas. In addition to his missionary work, Don worked for the Panama Canal. For a while he drove a dump truck in the building of Madden Dam; later he was the timekeeper in an office connected with that construction work. In 1934, under the leadership of Dr. Harold Chalfant, the Foursquare Crusaders (youth) in the United States began supporting monthly the missionary kids on the field who were involved in ministry. Donald was one of those who received a missionary allowance of twenty-five dollars a month. He was involved in full-time ministry, preaching, and teaching.

Miss Edith Sumrall and her mother began attending the Sunday services in the Frijoles church. They were from Mississippi and were Spirit-filled Christians. They lived in Cristobal, on the Atlantic side, where Edith was employed. A romance started between Edith and Donald, and, in June 1935, they were married in Gatun, Canal Zone. Dad performed the ceremony.

Beginning in 1934 my parents began to make frequent trips into the interior to Chitre, the fourth largest city of the country, about 160 miles from Panama City. They rented an adobe house with two front doors opening on to one of the plazas of the town and in which they began holding meetings. On one particular ministry trip, the American Bible Society colporteur, Mr. Halliday, accompanied my father. One night after service, there were several rowdies in the saloon next door. Dad decided to sleep on his cot in the open doorway in order to protect his car that was parked in front. Mr. Halliday sought more security and slept in a back room. In the middle of the night, Mr. Halliday, awakened by the noise in the saloon, decided to try to persuade Dad to close the door of the house, so they could be safe. But when he entered the front room and looked, he saw an angel standing at the head of Dad's cot with a drawn sword! Needless to say, Mr. Halliday went back to sleep, more than confident that all was well.

As I wrote earlier in these memoirs, in 1927, while Dad was a student in LIFE Bible College, he had a vision of an old man with a plow in a field looking for help. After arriving in Panama in 1928, Dad saw the man of his vision in the hospital and learned that he was a missionary from Chitre in the interior of the country. Because of those events, Dad wanted to start a Foursquare church in that city.

Mr. Latham, the man in the vision, had left his property to the Free Tract Society of Los Angeles, which in turn deeded it to the Foursquare Church in Panama. On the property was a one-room building, which had served as his dwelling place. It opened onto a plaza. A request for a building permit had sat on the desk of the city mayor for over two years. However, our attorney could not get any action from the city government. The city decided to construct a street across the lot. By the way, the street was never used and finally was covered with weeds.

In 1935 the Moncivaiz family moved to Chitre. The work was growing, and a resident missionary was needed to further establish that ministry and begin reaching outlying towns and villages in that part of the country. Frank and Juventina rented an adobe house with the native tile roof, typical of most buildings in that area. The living quarters were on one side with a large room that served for the church services on the other.

Frank and Juventina carried out the same type of ministry they had learned while working with my parents in Panama City. Dad was evangelistic in his preaching; my mother was gifted in teaching. Frank had a good teaching ministry, and Juventina was the evangelist. From the very start of the work, both ministries were used. The people received Jesus as Savior and were baptized in water as soon as possible; prayer services were conducted for people to receive the baptism with the Holy Spirit, and the Word was taught so they would become faithful followers of the Lord. Also, they would take two or three new believers with them when going to the villages to hold services. This gave these new Christians opportunities to lead the singing, give their testimonies, and begin preaching the Word. Dad was always getting people involved, giving them the liberty to minister. That was a way in which leaders were trained in the work.

The Moncivaizes started several churches in the interior of Panama, especially in the Herrera Province. It was a difficult field. There was much opposition to the gospel, and Frank's and Juventina's lives were threatened several times. But God was true to His Word; many were saved, many were healed miraculously, and many were filled with the Spirit. In 1943, when the board in Los Angeles appointed them to serve in Mexico, they left behind in Panama a well-established work.

Another successful church planter was Catalina Moran. The first time I met her was in our church in Guachapali, Panama City. She was saved there and filled with the Holy Spirit. Catalina was about five feet tall and was a real "powerhouse" for the Lord. Her eight-year-old son, Ruben, was always with her. It would be hard to find a more zealous witness for the Lord; she was always bringing new people to church to hear the gospel. As far as formal education was concerned, she had not had much. She knew how to read and write, and loved God's Word. Though she was of a quiet nature, she was an excellent communicator with a pleasing personality.

Catalina had attended every service for two or three years and then, suddenly, was gone without a word. That was the case more than once with Catalina. The first time was in 1935. She and little Ruben weren't seen or heard of for three to four months. Then suddenly, they were back and attending every service. When we questioned Catalina, we learned she and her son had gone about sixty miles into the interior of the country by bus to El Valle—a rural community away from the main road—which became their starting point. There they began to witness to people, giving out tracts, and holding services. This took place in the open air and, at other times, in homes of strangers who heard them and invited them to be their guests, eager to know more about God.

On this particular trip, they followed trails across mountains, fording rivers, and sleeping wherever they were welcomed. Most of the area they covered was very rural, with scattered adobe houses on small farms and villages. Although they established no churches, a large number from the countryside of the Cocle Province heard the gospel through Catalina's preaching as they went from place to place. Finally, Catalina and Ruben arrived in the capital city of the province and began to evangelize. To the Christian in Panama, "evangelize" meant to communicate the gospel to others in a way they could understand, whether to just one person or to several at a time. This time, Catalina was arrested and put in jail for "stirring up trouble."

Why was this charge made? It was because her message was not in line with the official religion. When questioned as to what authority she had to proclaim the gospel, she replied, "Jesus told His followers to preach the gospel to every creature. I am one of His followers." She spoke those words with the authority given to her by the Holy Spirit. The officials released her but commanded her to leave the area. She and her son returned to the church in Panama City and gave a glowing testimony of what God had done in that part of the country. Many had accepted the Lord and had been healed from various diseases.

When Hazel Granvoll later went to the Chiriquí province to pioneer the Foursquare church, she asked Dr. Edwards if there would be someone who would like to help her in the work. Dad sent Catalina, with her young son. She worked side by side with Hazel in the rented building where services were held in David, the capital city of that province. Yet, Catalina's heart was really out in the rural areas and villages. So she often made trips of several weeks at a time, making friends, leading people to Christ, and starting home meetings. Over a period of years, she started some sixty meeting places, and about thirty of those became Foursquare churches. She and her son finally settled in Puerto

Armuelles, a seaport for the United Fruit Company and started the church in Carcache, a suburb of that town. Many of the pastors of our churches in that part of the country that borders on Costa Rica owe their lives in Christ to Catalina Moran.

We tried various styles of evangelism, and they were often more effective than we dared hope. Driving to and from the interior, we would toss gospel tracts out of the car to pedestrians on the road. At least 95 percent would pick up the literature—even those riding on horseback would get down from their horses and pick up the tracts. Most of the time, we never knew the result of those efforts. But occasionally we would hear that people were brought to the Lord by that simple evangelistic activity. Such was the case of a man who attended one of the first services in Pajonal.

Gregorio Gutierrez was one of the men who had been saved and filled with the Spirit in the Caño Quebrado Church. He gained experience in leadership in that congregation and felt called of the Lord to move to the community of Pajonal. To get there, Gregorio took his family, with their belongings, by bus to the interior town of Penonomé. They walked several hours crossing rivers and climbing steep mountain trails. Gregorio began holding meetings in the adobe and thatched roof house of a family, not yet saved, that allowed him to do so.

In one of the very first gatherings, a man came forward with a tract that was yellow with age. He said to Gregorio, "Many months ago, I was walking along the highway far from here and some people in a car threw out this piece of paper. I picked it up, but not knowing how to read, I brought it home. My son, who knows how to read, read the paper to us. It is about the same God you speak about. Through the message of that piece of paper, I gave my heart to Jesus and I am so happy you have come to tell us more about God."

God blessed Gregorio's ministry, and many people in the area received Christ. A strong church resulted, and it touched that area of the country for miles around. The people built a very nice adobe church; the whole structure was of native materials. People came from far and wide to the services—many walking up to ten hours one way. And they were not disappointed, for God met them in those meetings. Many were saved, healed, and baptized with the Holy Spirit. The Word was the message they heard, and soon other areas that lay across other mountain streams began to hear the Good News.

I well remember, in my teens, driving to Penonomé and then hiking for several hours to Pajonal to stay in the home of Gregorio and to take part in the services. One time as we were walking, Gregorio asked me, "Do you know that Jesus prayed for me?" (See John 17:20.) Gregorio's love for his Lord was deep. As we walked the trail, we would come by little adobe homes and see people reading the Bible. Gregorio walked many miles and many hours with the gospel.

After our marriage, Barbara journeyed to Pajonal to minister to the congregation. During those times the people wanted services during the day and also far into the night. As many of them had traveled more hours on foot to get to the church than we had, they wanted as much teaching, prayer, and singing as possible.

10

◁ Our Second Furlough

IN AUGUST 1935 my parents were in need of a good rest. We learned of a Japanese shipping company with modern freight ships that frequently passed through the Panama Canal, coming from Japan and the West Coast of the United States on their way to the East Coast. The cost of the return trip from Panama to Los Angeles was forty dollars.

Dad wrote an airmail letter to the missions office in Los Angeles, stating that we had decided to take a furlough. He mailed it on our way to board the ship. It was an excellent voyage—good food, good accommodations, and a friendly crew. In those days, freighters often had accommodations for up to twelve passengers. The staterooms were very nice, and the food was excellent. Travelers ate their meals at the captain's table. Shortly after we had gotten underway and out to sea, one of the ship's stewards came to us and insisted on knowing at what hour each day each of us would have our bath. I cannot remember what time my parents agreed to, but I decided on three o'clock each day. The bathtub was of cement overlaid with marble, and the sides were about two and half feet high. It was almost big enough to accommodate a water baptismal service. The steward prepared the bath, filling the tub almost to the top. Then he went to find the person scheduled for it. No matter where I was, whether on the bow or in a deck chair reading a book, he would come, bow low, and tell me my bath was ready. We had such a pleasant voyage that, from that time on, whenever we traveled to the United States for furlough, we made the roundtrip on a freighter.

When the ship docked in San Pedro, California, we were met by Joe Henderson, a Foursquare missionary who had returned from the Belgian Congo. He drove us to Angelus Temple to the missions office where we received a warm welcome. Then we took the train to Morgan Hill, California, to be with family for a rest before going on an extensive itinerary to speak in Foursquare churches presenting the Foursquare missions program.

Dad purchased a secondhand car on monthly payments, and we left Los Angeles going east to Zion, Illinois, to visit my sister, Barbara, and her husband. While we were there, she gave birth to a cute little girl whom they named Ruth. In the Chicago area we spoke in a rally held in the Chicago Foursquare Church. Reverend Sidney Correll was in charge and coaxed me into speaking for a few minutes.

That was the first time I had spoken to an English-speaking audience. Before leaving Panama, I had begun preaching from time to time, of course, in Spanish. Prior to our furlough Dad had purchased a Keystone sixteen-millimeter movie camera for eighteen dollars, and in the services we started showing a short movie depicting some of the work in Panama. This was a first for Foursquare Missions.

Our itinerary took us into churches in Wisconsin and Illinois, among other states. Then we drove west to speak in Idaho, Oregon, Washington, British Columbia, and northern California on our way back to Los Angeles.

While in Portland, Oregon, I was asked to give the message to the Portland Crusaders (youth) in one of their services. The group was large but very attentive, and I enjoyed speaking to them about Panama and what God had done there.

Prior to leaving Panama, I had purchased all of the textbooks I would need for the first semester of my junior year in high school. While I was on furlough, I studied to keep up with my subjects. In the late fall, I attended Belmont High School in Los Angeles. After school, I went to the Free Tract Society in downtown Los Angeles and helped in the printing of literature. The director volunteered to print and make available free of charge as many copies of the Gospel of John in Spanish as we would need.

I learned to operate some of the machines, including the power cutter. I did most of the cutting on those booklets.

After the Foursquare convention, conducted at Angelus Temple in January 1936, we sailed back to Panama on another Japanese freighter. Along with our baggage, we also shipped over one ton of Gospel of John booklets. Our ship would not be docking in Balboa, but would pass through the Panama Canal and proceed up the east coast. We would disembark in a Panama Canal launch, the same one that brought the canal pilot out to the ship. Thus, the ship's captain radioed ahead, requesting a larger launch, stating our baggage was more than a ton. Neither the shipping company nor the Panama Canal charged us for loading and unloading what was really freight. God is good!

When I reported for class in Balboa, Canal Zone, only a week was left of the first semester. I was told that if I could pass all of the semester final exams I would receive the full semester credit for each class. The Lord helped me, and good grades were the result. It so happened that in taking the exam for advanced algebra, I didn't make a single mistake.

God had given us a good furlough. And we had much more waiting for us when we got back to the land of our calling.

11

◄ From Sea to Sea and Border to Border

AFTER THE WORK began to spread to other areas, beginning in the last half of 1928, Dad and Mother held special training sessions with the early converts. These are the people who became pastors and church leaders. As early as 1930, the first annual convention was held in the old wooden church building that we originally rented. The crowd was not very large, but it was the beginning of a church movement that over the next few years would spread across the entire nation. When my parents were appointed missionaries to Panama, their vision was to reach the entire country of Panama with the Foursquare gospel.

Many people, including businessmen and government officials, had told us that a needful step for the Foursquare Church in Panama was to acquire property and build a church structure in the national capital, Panama City. They said, "When that happens, we will know your church will be established and has come here to stay." We often prayed, as did the members in our churches, that God would provide a property that would become the headquarters for the Foursquare Church in the Republic of Panama.

Shortly after our arrival in Panama in the beginning of 1928, Dad and Mother became acquainted with the missionaries of the Free Methodist Church in Panama City. The church building was at the extreme end of the city. The church services were in English for the people who had come to Panama from the West Indies to work on the Panama Canal. The sanctuary was of concrete, had a corrugated iron roof, and seated about three hundred people. Attached to the back was a two-story wooden frame building. On the first floor there was a room for Sunday school and youth, as well as another room for an office. On the second floor were the living quarters for the missionaries. Next to this structure was a vacant lot of the same size that was part of the property owned by the church. Since the missionaries did not live there, our family rented the vacant living quarters for our home for a few months until the Free Methodist Church sent a new missionary unit to open a Spanish-speaking work. We then moved down the street about four blocks and rented another vacant house for our home.

In 1936 Dad learned that the Free Methodist Church had decided to close its work in Panama City. Negotiations started with the Free Methodist board in the United States to purchase that property. Finally, the purchase agreements were signed, with the sale price fixed at six thousand dollars. This was payable at the rate of one thousand dollars per year for six years, without interest. Of course, that was a lot of money at that time. We were so thankful that the international board of the Foursquare Church in Los Angeles approved the purchase and that the Foursquare churches in the United States raised the funds to make the payments.

Considerable repair work needed to be done, especially to the living quarters. Together with some of the men of our church who volunteered their time, we worked to do what was necessary to move into the property. The living quarters became our home. The two Foursquare congregations in the city united and moved into one church building that was now "theirs." For the first time, the Panama Foursquare Church had a field office. Words cannot fully describe the rejoicing and thanksgiving of our Panamanian Christians for their new church home. They now had ample space to carry out a more complete ministry: Sunday school, Sunday morning worship, Crusader (youth) meetings, nightly evangelistic and teaching services, prayer meetings, and, soon, a Bible institute.

One block away was Avenida Central, the main artery that

stretched from one end of the metropolis to the other end, and on which practically all of the bus lines had their routes. Our new property was on a corner, and the street passing the church from Avenida Central ended just three blocks away at the entrance of the national stadium.

The establishing of the headquarters property for the Foursquare Church in Panama in 1936 provided many necessary benefits. It was well located in the nation's capital, which was the center for government, commerce, education, and communication. The building provided an adequate auditorium for public meetings, a room that doubled for the Bible institute and Crusader youth, a smaller room for the church and national office, and living quarters for our family. With the national Headquarters Church and office, the reality of the vision to see the gospel extended throughout the nation was strengthened.

Quite often the evangelistic messages on Sunday nights in the Panama City church were vividly illustrated. With our little hand-operated mimeograph, we printed handouts advertising the service with an invitation to attend the meeting. These would be given in quantities to the members and adherents a few days before. They distributed them, generally one-on-one, and sometimes also with a gospel tract.

Clara Gallagher, "Hermana Clara," lived some distance from the city. She would ride the bus and a streetcar to church. Hermana Clara was a real witness for Jesus. She loved giving tracts and copies of the Gospel of John to other passengers. One particular day she handed a tract and invitation to a very hard looking woman who was barefooted. The woman said, "I cannot go to your church without shoes." So Sister Clara took her to a shoe store and bought her a pair of brand new shoes. That night Julia Tenorio received Jesus into her heart. God not only saved her but also healed her of tuberculosis in both lungs and delivered her from demonic possession.

Julia had been a prostitute, drug runner, and a very well-known witchdoctor. Some of her clients had been wealthy businessmen.

She was well paid to cast spells on the enemies of those who hired her, and she had become a woman feared by many. But with Jesus in her heart, she became a very different person. She began attending church services regularly. By being a good listener, she learned about the Lord and His Word. Although she had very little formal education, she was very zealous in witnessing to others, telling them how God had healed her and rescued her from a life of witchcraft and prostitution.

After a time, she left Panama City for the interior of the country and began sharing the gospel. In the rural area of La Mata and Pueblo Nuevo de Santiago in the Veraguas Province, the people she talked to about the Lord told her of a lady named Rosa de Aisprua. Rosa was in much need of help from God. She had been suffering for quite some time with a severe blood disease. She had been in and out of the hospital on several occasions. Julia told Rosa that Jesus Christ is the same today as He was back in Bible times. Julia prayed, and Rosa was instantly healed.

Many of the people of that vicinity gave their hearts to the Lord. More miracles took place, many were baptized with the Holy Spirit, and the new converts built a church out of native materials. The area had lots of petrified wood, and the walls of the church building were constructed of that material. Julia stayed there a few years pastoring that congregation. However, she felt led to pioneer in another area, so she went to the Chiriquí Province to the town of San Juan. Again, God blessed her ministry, with many coming to Christ and being healed and filled with the Spirit. Thus another church was raised up, along with several daughter churches.

The spread of the gospel always included the miraculous. In the early beginnings of the work in Pueblo Nuevo, my parents attended a service. Rosa's son, about four years old, had never been able to walk. Dad anointed him with oil in the name of the Lord and prayed for him, and God did a miracle. The little boy began to walk and was completely well in both legs. Soon he was running and jumping as though he had always been able to do so.

I remember clearly one event that happened several years later. It was the first night of the youth camp in Pueblo Nuevo for the churches of the central provinces, and I had asked Patricio Rodriguez, pastor of the church in Chitre, to be the speaker. He spoke on the subject of Jesus, the Great Physician. At the conclusion there were several that came forward to be prayed for. One of them was a young man named Pastor, another of Rosa's sons. Some time before, his horse had slipped and fallen on him. His leg was very badly broken. He had been in the hospital more than once for surgery on the leg. Finally, the doctor informed him that he would have to use crutches the rest of his life. After prayer that night, I asked him to leave his crutches and begin to walk. He did! The next afternoon he played in a soccer game, running back and forth the length of the field. During a visit with his sister in March 2001, Pastor came by on his horse and we had a nice chat. Forty-five years later, his legs were still very healthy!

In 1936 Hazel Granvoll came to Panama to help in the church. She had been a classmate of my parents in LIFE Bible College and had been active in evangelistic and pastoral ministries in the United States, mainly in the Midwest. She lived in our home while studying Spanish and took a definite part in the work, often preaching in Panama City and nearby congregations. She loved people and put herself wholeheartedly into reaching the lost for Christ. A year later, the board in Los Angeles formally appointed her as a missionary to Panama. After two years of gaining experience in the work, she felt called to go to the part of Panama that borders on Costa Rica, the Chiriquí Province, and start a Foursquare work in David, the third largest city in the country. We had gone by auto to David two or three times and Dad had the desire for a Foursquare church to be established there. The city was accessible by road, a trip of about three hundred miles. The pavement ended about halfway, and from there on it was a dirt road. The trip took two days, so we stayed overnight at a village church and conducted a service that night and continued on the next morning. The church that Hazel planted there made one section of our strategy complete: we had reached the major cities of Panama.

The Foursquare movement was now ministering in the four largest cities of the country: Panama City, Colon, David, and Chitre. Each of these centers then began to extend out to towns and villages in their surrounding areas, establishing churches that radiated from urban centers. The work in the Darien Province, bordering with Colombia, had been initiated in 1934. By the end of the 1930s, the message of the Foursquare gospel had extended from the Pacific to the Atlantic and from the northern border with Costa Rica to the southern border with Colombia.

12

◄ "Firsts" in Panama

THE FIRST FOURSQUARE Bible institute in Panama began in 1937, in the room in back of the church auditorium in Panama City. Classes were conducted four nights a week, and the initial number of students was approximately fifty. When the Bible institute was started in 1937, many were eager to become students in a more formal setting. They also participated in public ministry for practical training and became more effective in doing God's work.

The curriculum was laid out over three years, two semesters per year, and scheduled in keeping with the public school year, starting the last of March and ending just before Christmas. Because of lack of space—we had only one classroom—the school was on a three-year cycle. New students could begin at the beginning of any semester, but each subject would only be repeated every three years. It was not the ideal situation, but it had to suffice for a while.

In those days it was the custom for missionaries to establish Bible institutes in rural areas. Classes would be held in the morning, and the students would work on the land in the afternoon to raise food for the school. Dad was not impressed with that method. From his study of the Acts of the Apostles, my father recognized that Paul conducted his "institutes" in a center of population, commerce, education, and government, where the students would already be prepared to study and have the ability to communicate the gospel.

Dad, Mother, Hazel Granvoll, and I were the first teachers. My brother, Donald, and his wife, Edith, were on furlough in the United States. After returning to Panama, both of them also taught classes. I had been appointed as a Crusader Missionary in April of that year. My parents saved all of their study books and materials from LIFE Bible College. By the time I was halfway through high school, I had studied all of their syllabi and books, as well as other material. Much of the lesson material we used for the classes was translated into Spanish and typed on stencils. We made copies on our little hand-operated mimeograph.

In 1937 Thaddeus and Helen Tuttle, with their two small children, Carl and Carlene, arrived in Panama as Foursquare missionaries. Thaddeus had graduated from LIFE Bible College in the same class with my parents, and Helen a couple of years later. Both had been involved in pioneering and pastoring churches in the United States. After they had time to become oriented and study Spanish, they taught in the institute and served in other ministerial capacities in the work. Later they moved to Penonomé, a large town about a hundred miles west of Panama City, and pioneered a Foursquare church in that area.

After Donald left Panama to serve as supervisor of the Foursquare Church in the West Indies, Thad and his family moved to Colon and pastored the Colon congregation. They played a strong role in developing more churches throughout the Colon Province. They were good pastors and teachers, encouraging church leadership and winning many to Christ.

Thad and Helen had built a church building in Foursquare's Midwest District of the United States. They had also been sent to Mexico to construct the Headquarters Church in Monterrey. Many of our interior churches had grown and wanted to reconstruct their native built facilities, using cement block. In Panama the rainfall is heavy, often over one hundred inches a year, so foundations were very important. Thad helped us put in many foundations for churches all over the country.

The main ministry that I was involved in was to the youth. In those days Foursquare youth were called Crusaders. The first Crusader group to be organized in Panama was in 1935. The Crusader bylaws, as used in the United States, were translated into Spanish and adopted. Officers were elected by the youth of the church. The first president was a young high school student named Lionel Golbon.

When we made the move to the headquarters property, the Crusaders were happy to have their own room for their early Sunday evening meetings, held prior to the Sunday night evangelistic service. We received the monthly Crusader manual from Dr. Harold Chalfant's office in Los Angeles. I used it to publish a monthly manual in Spanish for our Crusader groups that were being started in the other Panama churches. It was not long before we began having Crusader rallies, and the church in Frijoles served as an ideal location for these get-togethers, since it was about half way between the two main terminal cities of the Panama Canal and was accessible by the railroad.

In the dry season of 1939 we held our first Crusader camp. Panama has two main seasons: the dry season extending from the last of December through March when it seldom rains; and the rest of the year, known as the rainy season. The camp was conducted in Penonomé for one week. It was something brand new for that part of the world. Several have told us that it was the first gospel youth camp held in Latin America.

We rented four houses made of adobe. Two were for the young ladies and two for the young men. These were not vacant, but the families occupying them gladly accepted a few dollars to live out in their backyards during that short time. All campers had to bring their own cots, hammocks, or sleeping mats and their own dishes. The cooks prepared the meals outdoors under the shade of a large tree. Breakfast consisted of a bowl of oatmeal, a micha (type of French roll), and coffee. Lunch was sancocho (soup consisting of meat and various vegetables), and rice. The evening meal was rice, beans and meat—generally beef.

Bible classes were held in the morning, culminating with the Holy Spirit class. This class included a teaching on the Holy Spirit and prayer for people to receive the baptism with the Holy Spirit. One of the other subjects taught was personal evangelism.

Many of the campers put into practice what they learned in that class and did one-on-one witnessing with the local residents. In the afternoon there were various sports events, mainly baseball and swimming. There was a wonderful area for bathing in the river not far away. A "victory circle" was held after the evening meal, giving opportunity for a time of sharing what the Lord had done in people's lives. The evening evangelistic service took place and people from around the town came to see what was happening. Several gave their hearts to the Lord.

One day, we decided to have a parade from one end of Penonomé to the other, marching down the main street. We had a few instruments, and the small number of musicians led the parade behind a person bearing the Panamanian flag. Then came all of the campers, giving out tracts along the entire distance and singing gospel songs and choruses that were being played by the band.

Another first had to do with radio. Owning a radio was very common in Panama. Whether the home was large or small, in the poorer sections or the more privileged, even in virtually every saloon, there was a radio. As soon as people awakened in the morning, the radio was turned on, and it wasn't turned off until everyone had gone to bed at night. Because of the tropical weather, windows and doors were open and the sounds from the radio could be heard everywhere. In 1943 we began our first broadcast on the Radio Miramar longwave station. The program was broadcast every Sunday morning. As far as we know, it was the first Christian radio program in the Spanish language in Panama.

The studio was located on the waterfront in the Bella Vista section of Panama City. We organized a group of young people from our Calle Q Church to sing and give testimonies. God gave us a young man with a beautiful tenor voice. I had known him since he was a babe in arms. His parents and other members of his family came to the Lord in the church in Agua Bendita (Chilibre). Santiago Stevenson thrilled our listeners with his outstanding voice, singing on our programs. He was known as El Trovador Evangélico (The Gospel Troubadour). The radio program was called La Iglesia del Aire (Church of the Air). The broadcast was one half hour in length, starting with a chorus: "Paz y Reposo Tengo en Jesús, no mas tinieblas, ando en la luz; El va conmigo, que felicidad; El es mi amparo por la eternidad" (I have peace and rest in Jesus; no more darkness, I walk in the Light; He walks with me, what wonderful happiness; He is my refuge for all eternity). This was followed by a lively hymn, generally with the Latin rhythm, church announcements very briefly done, and a special musical number by one member of our group. Then I gave a twelve-minute message ending with an invitation to receive the Savior.

Because of World War II, everything we said on the program had to be typewritten; two copies were taken to the government office to be approved by a censor. We could use no numbers such as chapter and verse. The censor's office kept a copy and the original was duly stamped and signed and was the script used in the broadcast. This method proved to be another avenue to meet more people. Since they had to read the manuscript, more folks got the gospel. Of course, after the war was over, the censorship stopped.

Over the years we broadcast programs on several radio stations. We had no problem getting a station to accept us, and the ministry became very popular. One of our aims was to broadcast on a station that was popular in the saloons as well as in homes. We desired to reach those who were without Christ. Most of our broadcasts were on Sunday in the late afternoon. All the broadcasts were live.

Toward the end of the 1940s, another new powerful shortwave radio station was built in Panama City. We bought time on it and aired our program each Monday night. We received letters from various countries throughout Latin America. One letter came from a congregation in Venezuela. At that time they had no pastor, so, when our program came on, the people gathered in their church and placed a radio on the pulpit. Our broadcast became their weekly meeting.

One Sunday night, when the altar call was given at the conclusion of the message in the Calle Q Church (also known as Central Church or Headquarters Church), a man came seeking the Lord. His wife had left him, taking their child with her. He was despondent and had decided to take his life. As he opened the dresser drawer to take out a gun to end his life, he turned on the radio and heard our program. His heart was touched; he realized there was hope for him. He came to the church and gave his life to Christ.

Over time we learned of many who came to the Savior through listening to La Iglesia del Aire. Doors were opened for other ministries. A Catholic priest, who had left his robes to get married, heard the broadcast. He was the director of secondary education for the country of Panama. He came personally to our office, seeking the Lord. That interview opened a series of events that led to a meeting with a president of Panama who had been in exile. He heard the gospel and repeated a prayer of acceptance of the Lord.

As we look back, we continue to praise the Lord that these "firsts" were not "lasts." Those programs that were started decades ago are still continuing, yet in adapted forms and methods relevant to the Panamanian culture today.

13

◁ Four Very Special Visitors

Missionaries love visitors who come and see the field firsthand. It is uncanny how missionaries and their families can recall those visits and even the dates they occurred. Above the rest, however, there are those very special visitors who leave a lasting imprint upon the field.

In 1939, Aimee Semple McPherson, the founder and president of the International Church of the Foursquare Gospel, came to Panama. She was the guest of our family. Accompanying her on this trip were Dr. and Mrs. Giles Knight. Dr. Knight was vice president of the denomination. Sister McPherson was greatly used by God to preach about the ministry of the Holy Spirit. Wherever she preached, people experienced fresh spiritual outpourings. Tens of thousands of people around the world came to Christ, were healed of many diseases and afflictions, and were baptized with the Holy Spirit with the evidence of speaking in tongues.

Sister McPherson came to Panama to visit the Panamanian people in the Foursquare churches and to enjoy fellowship with them. She was in Panama for one week, preaching each night and twice on Sunday, and each time in a different church. At her request, no advance publicity was made through the news media. She had not come to hold a campaign. Yet people were saved and many were healed in the meetings. Everyone was happy to meet her and to hear her speak.

Her first service was in the Headquarters Church in Panama City. The church was packed to capacity before the service began. Her love and compassion for people were very evident. She ministered in Agua Bendita, located about seventeen miles from Panama

City. We took her to Chitre in the interior of the country where she also preached. Early on Sunday morning we drove out to Gamboa and took a launch across the Gatun Lake to Caño Quebrado, a village where the entire population had accepted the Lord and were members of the Foursquare church. All of us had a great time worshiping the Lord. People had come from all around to hear her speak, and they were not disappointed.

When Sister McPherson came to Panama I was in my late teens, and I had the privilege of interpreting for her in several of the services. She also took time to have some good talks with me. We talked about the Lord, the ministry, sports, and everyday life. One afternoon, at her request, I took her in our little Willys car downtown in Panama City. She teased me saying she could park her big car better than I could the little one. Leaving the car we walked along Central Avenue. She took me into a men's shop and had me try on a white linen suit. She said that she wanted to buy it for someone my size. Back in the car, she gave me the package containing the suit she had bought, saying she had purchased it for me. For a long time after that I would wear that suit to preach, and it became a reminder of the love, kindness, and humility of Sister McPherson, who was so anointed by God. I will always be grateful that she set aside time to show interest in a young man such as me.

I had not received the baptism with the Holy Spirit, yet had been earnestly seeking that experience. As Sister McPherson was boarding the train to go to the Atlantic side to board the ship to return to the United States, there on the observation platform she urged me, with much love, to press on and receive God's promised power with the evidence of speaking in tongues. A few months later, while on furlough, I attended a series of meetings in the Burbank, California Foursquare Church. There, under the ministry of Reverend Ethel Heidner, I was filled with the Holy Spirit and have enjoyed the "promise of the Father" and the beauty of spiritual language until today. That was sixty-five years ago, and it is still as fresh today as it was back then.

Following World War II, we were thrilled to have Dr. Rolf K. McPherson, president of the International Church of the Foursquare Gospel and son of our founder, Aimee Semple McPherson, as a guest speaker at one of our annual national conventions. He faithfully carried out the vision of his mother—to reach the nations with the gospel message. As he told what God was accomplishing around the world through the Foursquare movement, our faith and vision were strengthened. Long after his visit, pastors and members recalled and rehearsed with others the testimonies he had shared.

From 1944 through 1949, Dr. Howard P. Courtney, Sr., served as director of foreign missions. He made two trips to Latin America. He spent several days with our family in Panama, and he spoke in several of the churches in various parts of the country. On one occasion, I invited all of the Foursquare missionaries to come together for a time of prayer and fellowship. I remember Dr. Courtney speaking to us out of his heart regarding the necessity of being filled anew with the Holy Spirit. It was a landmark experience for each of us who needed a fresh touch from God.

In 1950 Dr. Herman D. Mitzner became the missions director. He served in that office for fifteen years. Most of all, Dr. Mitzner was a spiritual father to all the missionaries. One of his favorite verses was Colossians 4:6: "Let your speech be always with grace, seasoned with salt, that ye may know how ye ought to answer every man" (KJV).

Dr. Mitzner visited Panama on two different occasions. Each time, he spoke in several of the churches as well as over the radio. And each time he asked, "How long has it been since someone has been baptized with the Holy Spirit in your ministry?" I was always glad that I could inform him that people had been received that glorious experience within the last week before his arrival.

We were blessed to have such wonderful leaders, people who loved and prayed for us. What a privilege it was for Barb and me to be able to join them at Foursquare headquarters in 1960 and serve with them for many years.

14

◁ Only on the Mission Field

E VERY MISSIONARY HAS stories, and I am no different. Read, rejoice, and enjoy.

MAMA MECHA'S TWO BAPTISMS

The Sunday morning train from Colon, Panama, brought several passengers to the village of Frijoles. Having heard of what God was doing in the Frijoles Foursquare Church, most of them had come seeking physical healing. One was an elderly lady known by all of her friends as Mama Mecha. That morning Mama Mecha, along with several others, received Jesus as Savior and wanted to take the next step of being baptized in water. Just a short distance from the church was an inlet of the Gatun Lake. Each Sunday the new converts were baptized. Before being immersed, she gave a ringing testimony of having been born again. As she came out of the water, she lifted her hands in praise to the Lord and suddenly she began to speak in another language.

Standing in the crowd witnessing the service was a man from Spain. He had been an archeologist in Egypt for several years and had also served as a Roman Catholic priest in Spain and Panama. That late afternoon, while on the train returning to Panama City, he said to my parents, "That elderly woman, after being baptized, spoke in an ancient Egyptian language and quoted a psalm of praise from the Old Testament. There is no way she could even speak one word in that language which I learned in my work as an archeologist in Egypt. That had to be God." Dad explained to him that she was being baptized with the Holy Spirit according to Acts 2:4. It left a lasting impression in the heart and mind of this man. Mama Mecha served the Lord for many years in our church in Colon, leading many people to Christ.

A VERY UNUSUAL CHRISTMAS EVE

It was Christmas Eve. My father and I had driven out of Panama City to the end of the road toward Colombia in South America. We were there for the Christmas program in the Foursquare church in the village of Chepo. The building had three double windows, six-feet-tall on each side, always open during the service because of the hot weather.

There were many parts to the program: the first half of the evening consisted of recitations and skits by the children. Before the adult drama, there was a break; refreshments (coffee and hot chocolate) had been prepared for all.

Dad and I decided to take some pictures of those in the program, so everyone stayed in the church to watch us. The building was packed, with little standing room left. We asked all of the performers to go to the platform; they were the subjects for the pictures.

This happened back in the days when flash bulbs for taking night pictures were very new. But the flash would not work. We changed batteries, but with no success. In that town the electric current was 220 volts. Just above where we had the camera on the tripod was a wire hanging down with a white bulb in it, one of the lights for the church. I took out that bulb and screwed in the flash bulb (The early flash bulbs were the same size as regular light bulbs.). I held the reflector behind it while Dad tended the camera. When I turned the switch at the socket, there was a terrible flash. Then it was dark; the lights had gone out! People began running. Mothers with babies in their arms jumped through the windows. Everyone left the church through the nearest available escape route. Only the pastor, Dad, and I were left in the church.

When the people looked back from outside, they saw there had been no damage. Enemies of the gospel had predicted that lightning would strike the church and destroy it, and people thought that was the reason for the flash. We were thankful that no one was injured. They all came back in laughing, and the program went on as planned.

A MIGHTY WIND

The Pearl Islands are located in the Gulf of Panama about ninety miles south of the Pacific entrance to the Panama Canal. A tribe of Indians originally inhabited this archipelago for many centuries prior to the conquest by the Spanish. When Vasco Nunez de Balboa, standing atop the summit of Mount Pirre in the Darien Province of Panama, discovered the Pacific Ocean, he could see in the distance a group of islands—the Pearls. History relates that he demanded from the chief a large basin full of pearls.

It became the vision of Estanislao Urriola to take the message of the Pearl of Great Price to the inhabitants of those islands. He had a knack for doing the final artistic work in building construction and was always in demand. Before he found Christ, He had been deep in sin, spending his life in the sensual pleasures of unrighteousness. Friends brought him to our church in Panama City, and, at the end of the message when the altar call was made, he came forward to give his heart to the Lord. After leaving the service, he said out loud to himself, "I never want to go back to that place again." But a day or two later while he was at work, suddenly he was overwhelmed by the joy of the Lord. He raised his hands to God in thanksgiving for the forgiveness of his sins and the gift of eternal life. Estanislao continued to come to the church and learn more about his Savior and Lord. In a prayer service he received the baptism with the Holy Spirit and enrolled in our Bible school.

After graduation, Estanislao felt the call to enter into full-time ministry to pioneer in some area where the gospel had not been preached. However, a large problem surfaced. In consultation and prayer with him, we learned that in those places he was considering for his ministry were women whom he had already lived with. He would be like a "prophet without honor" in those locations. (See Matthew 13:57.) From the time of his conversion, however, Estanislao had become faithful and true to his wife. The door that God opened for them was the Pearl Islands. The Panama City church sent them, and a Sunday school class in the Burbank, California, Foursquare Church helped them financially. One of the items they sent money for was a cayuco (dugout canoe) to be used to go from island to island with the good news. A work on the main island of Isla del Rey was established, and services were held in villages in other parts of the archipelago.

After the work had started, Foursquare missionary Claude Updike and I took a small boat over to the islands. We wanted to visit the work and hold services in three different towns. We had concluded our visit to the Pedro Gonzalez Island and were to cross over to Isla del Rey before returning to Panama City. It was open ocean from island to island, and we were making the journey in Estanislao's dugout, "powered" by sail. The wind grew stronger, and, before long, we were in the midst of a vendaval (or, gale-force gusting winds). The boat was filling with water as fast as we could bail. I said to Claude, "I hope somebody is praying for us."

Finally the wind blew us up on a beach of a very small island. We were soaked to the skin. We got out of the boat, awfully glad to be on terra firma again, and we saw a man come running from one of the grass huts that dotted the beach. He was all excited and gave me un fuerte abrazo (a strong hug). A few months before, he had gone to Panama City to visit family and had been taken to our church where he had received the Lord into his heart. Two of his prized possessions were a Bible and hymnbook that he had purchased in Panama City. He begged us, "Please hold a service right here on the beach, now!" So we did. There were a total of six grass huts on the island, and several persons gathered with us to sing, listen to the Word, and have a time of prayer. By the time we finished, the storm had abated. We were able to launch out again into the deep and get back to Isla del Rey in time for the evening service in the town of San Miguel.

Looking back on that day, I realized that God sent a storm to cause us to be unexpectedly tossed up on that particular island. He had already prepared the way for the gospel through one man, one of God's children, who needed our help and encouragement to share the gospel with his neighbors.

Several days later, we received a letter from my mother-in-law, Gladys Noyes, in Burbank. The Lord had awakened her early on the day of the storm, telling her to pray for my safety because I was in danger. With the time difference of three hours between Panama and California, it was the very time we were in struggling in the boat. We later learned that Claude's wife, Juanita, and my wife, Barb, also were moved upon by the Lord to pray for us, not knowing our situation. The Lord had protected us even though he had sent a storm to direct us to the small island where we shared the story of Jesus.

JUVENCIO

Sitting in a *piragua* (a Choco Indian canoe), along the banks of the Chucunaque River in Panama, I was talking to Juvencio, one of our young Bible institute students. The two of us had come down the coast on a boat from Panama City and were headed up a major river in the Darien Province to conduct services in some of our churches. I never traveled alone; it was our policy to take national workers, some of them students, on various ministry trips. This provided excellent experience in the work of the Lord. We had tied up the piragua under the shade of a large tree, taking a short break between services in the nearby church. I asked Juvencio how he had come to know the Lord. What I heard was amazing!

Juvencio grew up in a small adobe house, up in the mountains from the town of Penonomé, in the central province of Cocle. One day, his father had traveled to Penonomé to purchase supplies. While in the large public market, he was handed a Gospel of John and a tract by our missionary, Thaddeus Tuttle, who lived in that town with his family. This was just one of those times when Thad was passing through the market passing out gospel literature. Juvencio's father knew how to read. That night, having returned home, he began reading the Gospel of John to his family. They read through the little booklet a couple of times. Then Juvenico's father learned that a friend of his, living several hours away, owned an entire Bible.

Juvencio was sent off on horseback to borrow "the Book." According to Juvencio, it took most of one whole day to get to the village and another day to return home. But each evening the entire family would gather to hear their father read from the Bible under the light from a kerosene lamp. After several weeks, Juvencio was directed to return the Bible to its owner. Interestingly, when the father had felt that sufficient time had elapsed so it would be appropriate to borrow "the Book" again, Juvencio would make another round trip. They had a hunger to learn more from the reading of God's Word. This happened many times.

When Juvencio, his brother, and sister had reached the age to leave home, their father sent them to Panama City to find work. He also handed them the gospel tract that had the address of the Foursquare church in Panama City printed on it. In fact, their father "ordered" them to find the church and attend. On one of their first visits to the church, the three of them received the Lord and, in time, became active members. Later, Juvencio studied in the Bible institute, graduated, and entered into full-time ministry.

Arthur F. Edwards

Edith (Breton) Edwards

Arthur and Edith Edwards

Leland and Barbara (Noyes)
Edwards in1941, shortly after
their marriage in Panama

The Edwards family prior to departure for Panama in1928;
l-r: Edith, Donald, Arthur, Leland, and Barbara

Donald and wife, Edith, with
U.S. serviceman stationed in
Panama

Dr. and Mrs. Arthur Edwards with Bible school
students in 1945

Aimee Semple McPherson's visit to Central Church,
Panama City, 1939

First pastor's convention in Panama, 1930; Edwards
family (center)

Central Church in Panama City, 1940

Central Church in Panama City, today

Pajonal Foursquare Church

Pajonal "stroller"—mother
carrying child on her back

Church of the Air radio program ministry team,
September 1945

Edith Edwards' Sunday School Class in Panama City,
1928; Leland (far right) in sailor suit

Rosendo de Orta with a deaf
and dumb boy who was healed
in Frijoles through prayer
by Edith Edwards, 1928

Gentleman in the interior
of Panama who asked, "But
what about my ancestors who
never heard?"

Chiriqui youth camp in 1950s

Harmodio Palacio taking the
gospel to the interior regions
of Panama, 1930

Catalina Moran with son,
Reuben

Rev. and Mrs. Luther Plankenhorn visit home of
Mr. Latham, 1935

Arthur Edwards with his 1925 Studebaker, which was
shipped to Panama

Leland Edwards doing "real" missionary work—
repairing his truck on the road

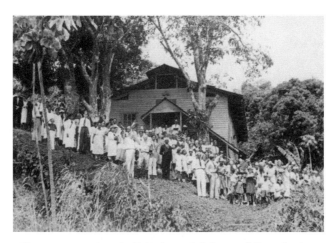

The congregation in Frijoles with Dr. and Mrs. Arthur
Edwards, 1931

Guaymi Indian family, July 1949

Leland and Barbara's sons:
Arthur (Duke) Edwards and
Loren (Butch) Edwards, with
pet parrot "Mac" in 1956

Typical church building in the interior of Panama

Typical church building in the interior of Panama

Typical church building in the interior of Panama

Leland Edwards with Choco Indians, 1949

l-r: Harmodio Palacio; Chicheme with wife and children; Claude Updike, Leland Edwards in the Darien Province, 1950

15

◁ Entrusting the Message

FROM THE VERY start of their ministry in Panama, my parents expected God to raise up church leaders from among the people, those who would give their hearts to the Lord and be filled with His Spirit. My parents' vision was to reach the entire country with the gospel. For that to happen would require that most of the ministry be accomplished through national ministers and local church leaders.

Dad was evangelistic in his preaching, and my mother was a good Bible teacher. God put their gifts to work, and signs followed the preaching and teaching of the Word. Dad and Mother taught that new believers should be baptized in water as soon as possible, even on the same day as their conversion. The one requirement was that they must have given their hearts to the Lord. As they stood in the water to be baptized, each person gave a personal testimony of having been saved.

Baptismal services were held outdoors in a river, lake, or wherever there was enough water. Many from the villages or towns came out of curiosity to see what was taking place. Often onlookers gave their hearts to the Lord, hearing the testimonies of those being baptized. In many areas, when friends, family, and onlookers saw a person being baptized, they knew that person had started a new walk of faith.

Rosendo de Orta was healed and saved in the first service held in the town of Frijoles in July 1928. He and his brother, Santos, said that, if we would return the next Sunday, they would go over the whole area and tell people what they had heard, seen and felt. They kept their word. The following Sunday, people had come from all around the region. Soon after the outpouring of the Holy

Spirit upon the early believers that year, my parents began taking Rosendo and others with them to various towns. This gave them opportunity to testify, lead the singing, and preach. They often led Bible studies and prayer meetings.

Rosendo and his wife, Carmen, were leaders in the church at Frijoles for several years. Soon after World War II, the Trans-Isthmian Highway was opened from Panama City to Colon (from coast to coast), and many migrated from various areas, starting farms and industry along its route. Rosendo and his family moved to the community of Quebrada Grande. There he started a Foursquare church and pastored it for several years.

Lionel Golbon was saved in the church in Guachapali (Panama City) in the early 1930s. He was in his teens and became a leader among the youth. It was in that church that the first local youth group was organized (Foursquare Crusaders). He was the first president. Lionel became a teacher in the high school in Panama City, a position he kept until retirement many years later. He served as a leader in the Headquarters Church, teaching Sunday school. He graduated from the Bible institute and later was on the staff as a teacher and sometimes preached in the services. Because of his bilingual ability, he often interpreted for visiting speakers who did not know Spanish.

Pedro Román came to the Lord in the church on Calle Q, the Headquarters Church. Soon his entire family was converted. He was a very faithful leader in that church for many years. He graduated from the Bible institute and often accompanied my parents to other towns and cities, taking part in the services and preaching. He was employed as a linotypist by the Panama America Newspaper Company. His wife, Petita de Román, became a prominent leader among the women in the church. She, too, graduated from the Bible institute and for many years faithfully taught the ladies Bible class in the Calle Q Church.

Patricio Rodriguez and his wife, Alicia, gave their hearts to the Lord in the Panama City Church, graduated from the Bible institute and were strong leaders in that congregation. He worked for the dredging division of the Panama Canal. He was the captain of a small boat in the canal that was used to keep the canal channel clean of debris. He was soon eligible for retirement, but did not delay the call of God upon his life. Patricio resigned his position and went to the interior of Panama, taking his wife and daughter. He pastored the church in Chitre and served for many years as the supervisor of the churches in the Herrera Province. Under his leadership several churches were pioneered.

Abraham Guardia and his wife, Daniela, were saved in the early years of the church in Pajonal. They later moved to Panama City and attended the Calle Q Church and graduated from the Bible institute. God called them to go to the Veraguas Province, where they pastored the church in Pueblo Nuevo de Santiago. Abraham eventually served as supervisor of the Veraguas Province, and under his leadership several churches were pioneered. Abraham and Daniela were the first pastors of the Santiago de Veraguas church.

Luis A. Harris D. and his wife, Sofia, attended the Calle Q Church and graduated from the Bible institute. Luis ("Lucho") was saved as boy in the Agua Bendita church and Sofía in the Calle Q Church, where they met and were married. They moved to the Chiriquí Province and pastored the church in El Volcan and then moved to Jacú, pastoring the church there. Lucho and Sofía pioneered several churches in Chiriquí, and Luis later served as supervisor of that province for several years before being appointed national supervisor for all of Panama. At the 1997 International Foursquare Convention in Cincinnati, Ohio, the International Church of the Foursquare Gospel awarded Luis an honorary doctor of divinity degree.

Pablo Bryson was saved in the church in Colon and became a leader in that church. He assisted in extending the work into other parts of the Colon Province. For a time he pastored the English-speaking church in Rainbow City, Canal Zone. He later moved north to the eastern part of the United States.

As a young girl, Telma Rivera de Carrera came to know the Lord in the Calle Q Church. Feeling the call to the ministry she went to Los Angeles, where she attended LIFE Bible College. Following graduation, she returned to Panama to be a leader in the work. She pioneered the church in Las Ollas and also taught in the Bible institute.

Ernesto Murillo was saved in the Calle Q Church and graduated from the Bible institute. God had gifted him with evangelism, and he held many crusades throughout Panama and several other Central American countries. He pioneered and pastored a church near Panama City and assisted in starting other churches in the Panama Province. He later was appointed the national supervisor for all of Panama.

Santos Vergara was also converted in the Calle Q Church, and he became a leader in that congregation. His wife had been saved in the meetings in Frijoles, but, at that time, he wanted nothing to do with the gospel. His wife continued to live the Christian life and attend the Calle Q Church. He saw in her a true example of what a Christian should be. He also saw families in the area who were now living changed lives, having been delivered from a life of sin to following Jesus. One night he followed her to church and sat in the back. She did not know that he was there until she saw him pass by in the aisle on his way to the altar to accept the Lord. He graduated from the Bible institute, gained experience by participating in services in nearby towns, and then went to the Los Santos Province. There he conducted outdoor meetings that were attended by thousands.

Margarita de García received the Lord as her Savior in the Calle Q Church one Sunday night. When Barbara gave the altar call at the end of her message, eleven members of one family, the Dominguez family, came forward. Margarita was one of them. She became a real fine worker in the church, graduated from the Bible institute, and later became one of the teachers in the institute. She pioneered and then pastored for several years the Foursquare church on Avenida A.

There are many more that could be written about: Sergiolina de Lescure, Aguedo Ortiz, Victor Rengifo, Lita de Cajar, Guillermo

Reales, Angélica and Lilia McPherson, Julia Panay, Carlos Cedeno, Carlos Contreras, Francisco de Soto, Cayetano Ortega, Juvencio Perez. It is not possible to tell all of the stories of these and many others who took the gospel to the nation of Panama.

From the beginning of the Foursquare Church in Panama in 1928, the Great Commission was taught. My parents let the people know God had called them to leave their home to take the gospel to Panama and God would lead people in Panama to take the gospel to other nations as well. What follows is stories of some of those who left Panama to become missionaries in foreign countries.

Harmodio Palacio, after pioneering the church in Caño Quebrado, left in the early 1930s. His trip took him by coastal boat to El Real in the Darien Province, and from there he hiked over land across the national border into Colombia. He started three churches along the Atrato River, later returning to Panama to pastor the church he had pioneered, and finally returned to the Darien Province to start several congregations.

Obdulio Estupiñán was converted in the Colon church in the early 1940s under the ministry of my brother, Donald. He graduated from the Bible institute in that church and assisted Donald in the ministry in Colon and neighboring towns. He was originally from Colombia and returned to Bucaramanga where he assisted the Paul Andersons in the work. From there he went to San Cristobal, Venezuela, under contract as a mechanic in a truck and auto shop. He pioneered the Foursquare work in that city, starting meetings in his home. One day a truck driver who was very opposed to his ministry intentionally ran Obdulio over in his shop. But Obdulio ministered to his small congregation from his bed until he died.

I remember that my father received a letter from his wife, asking for someone to take up "the torch." Dad passed the word on to the international board in Angelus Temple, and missionaries were sent to Venezuela.

Erasmo Escudero was saved under the ministry of Harmodio

Palacio in Yaviza, Darien, Panama. As a young man he moved to Panama City and attended the Calle Q Church, graduating from the Bible institute. His bilingual ability gave him an open door to serve as an interpreter for Claude Updike in his evangelistic campaigns in the early 1950s in various areas of Panama. Later when Claude and Juanita went to Costa Rica, Claude asked Erasmo and his wife, Ana, to help in the meetings by serving as his interpreters. One of the campaigns was held in Puntarenas, Costa Rica. A church was started out of the meetings, and Erasmo and Ana stayed to pastor that church for several years. Later they returned to Panama to pastor churches in their homeland.

Antonio Rojas was led to the Lord by Catalina Morán when she held meetings in La Pita, Province of Chiriquí. Antonio really loved the Lord and became a leader in the church in his area. He made many trips across the border into Costa Rica and started several Foursquare churches in towns in the banana zone. Over several years he nurtured them, and, under his ministry, God raised up several fine church leaders in that area. One of them was a young Guaymi Indian, Luisa. She started the work among the Guaymis in Panama and Costa Rica.

As a young boy, Victor Tejera began attending the Calle Q Church and was led to the Lord by his Sunday school teacher, Minerva de Chang. He graduated, still in his late teens, from the Bible institute and began his ministry assisting in that church and nearby churches. The door opened for him to go to Colombia and assist in the Foursquare work in that country. In the mid-1950s, because of his bilingual ability, Victor interpreted in Claude Updike's evangelistic meetings in Costa Rica, Nicaragua, and Honduras. Later, when the Updikes moved from Panama to Guatemala to pioneer the work in that country, Victor went along with them and was their interpreter for several years. He served as associate pastor of the Headquarters Church in Guatemala City. Victor married Rosemarie Anderson of Guatemala City. They later immigrated to California, where they entered the ministry and pastored a church in Chino for several years.

Esilda Mikalunakos de Silva came to the Lord in the Colon church and soon became a leader among the young people of that congregation. Later she went to Los Angeles with Telma Rivera from the Calle Q Church and enrolled in LIFE Bible College. After graduation, Esilda and Telma returned to Panama, and Esilda became the pastor of the Colon congregation. God blessed her ministry in that city. She had a strong evangelistic ministry, and, more than once, Claude Updike had her assist in his evangelistic meetings in Central America.

In the late 1950s, Jose Silva came to Panama from Colombia, looking for the girl God would have him to marry. He stayed with us in our home in Panama City for several months. He and Esilda met and were married. Later they became pastors of the Calle Q Church. For the last several years they have lived in Miami, Florida, where Jose is pastor of a large Spanish-speaking congregation.

Pablo Florez gave his heart to the Lord in the Colon church when he was just a boy. He became a leader with the youth, and, while attending the Bible institute, he helped Thaddeus and Helen Tuttle in meetings in various areas of the Colon Province. He later returned to his birthplace in Colombia and pioneered and pastored one of the largest Foursquare churches in that nation. Several congregations were started through his ministry. Years later he and his wife and family returned to Panama to pastor the Calle Q Church in Panama City.

Cristobal Cáceres accepted Jesus as Savior in the Calle Q Church. He was very faithful to the Lord in serving Him in the church and in churches in the area. He graduated from the Bible institute and went to Ecuador in the late 1950s to assist the Arthur Gadberrys in the work in Guayaquil. He then moved to a large town several miles away to pioneer a church and served as its pastor for many years.

As we look back over the work of these wonderful servants of the Lord, we find the continuation of 2 Timothy 2:2. Those to whom my parents entrusted the gospel truly were "able to teach others also."

16

◁ Doing the Work of an Evangelist

F ROM THE START of the Foursquare Church in Panama in
1928, evangelism played a major role. The vision was to
reach the entire nation with the gospel. To do so meant
winning people to Christ, teaching them God's Word and showing them how to apply it to their everyday lives.

Reaching the entire nation of Panama also required that those
being discipled share "the Message." When the believers received
the baptism with the Holy Spirit, they were more zealous to take
the good news to others. Personal evangelism was taught not
only in our churches but also in the youth and family camps.
God raised up pastors, teachers, and evangelists from the local
people and sent out missionaries empowered with various ministry gifts.

In the 1950s three well-known evangelists came to Panama,
and God gave them a very effective ministry. In 1951 Evangelist
T. L. Osborne came to the city of Colon to conduct a crusade
in the Colon Arena, a large sports arena seating around four
thousand people. It was packed every night, with many people
receiving the Lord due to the miracles of healing that took place.
I served as his interpreter during that crusade.

News of what was happening spread quickly to many areas.
Late one afternoon, Claude Updike looked down from the
little balcony of his apartment across the street from the
Calle Q Church in Panama City and saw the street literally
filled with people. They knew the Foursquare church practiced praying for the sick and afflicted. He went down to the
church, opened the doors, and soon no standing room was
left inside. He started a service in which many miracles took

place, and while the meetings continued in the Colon Arena, God did miracles in Panama City, night after night. Claude and Juanita Updike had come to Panama in 1948. They had pastored in northern California after graduating from LIFE Bible College. Claude was gifted in evangelism, and Juanita was especially gifted in children's ministry. We kept them busy carrying out those ministries in many parts of the nation.

In 1956 Evangelist Roberto Espinosa came to Panama City for a crusade. I was asked if I could help find a large vacant area on which to hold the meetings. The ideal place was a large vacant lot covering an entire block, about a half mile from the Calle Q Church. After inquiring as to who the owner was, I went to see him in his office. He owned so much land that he asked one of his secretaries to look into the files to make sure he was the owner of that lot. I told him I wanted to rent the property for one month. He replied, "I know who you are and the good work you are doing and will let you have it free of charge." I thanked him for the offer, but assured him that we intended to pay for the use of the lot. He said we could have it for three hundred dollars. I told him we would pay twenty-five balboas (dollars). I wrote out a check for that amount and requested a signed receipt, which he gave me. According to law, two permits were required for the open-air crusade. I went to the police and then to the mayor's office and secured both permits.

Finally, the arrangements were complete and the meetings began. On the second night, a man from the interior of Panama with a withered hand and arm that he could not use was instantly healed. The next day the main daily newspaper ran the story, four columns wide, down the entire length of the front page. I learned later that, on that day, the newspaper sold twice the usual number of copies. The crowds swelled to some twenty thousand and God did miracles every night. Best of all, hundreds gave their hearts to the Lord. Everywhere in the city people were talking about what was happening at the "Relleno de Balboa" which was what that area of the city was called.

A couple of days later, the daily newspaper ran a front-page picture of the evangelist, along with an interview. The question asked during the press interview was, "Does God heal?" Evangelist Espinosa stated emphatically that He does, and he provided numerous testimonies of the sick and afflicted being healed. After several more nights of services, with signs following the preaching of the Word, the authorities advised me that the evangelist was officiating without the proper documents. We hired a lawyer and went to the mayor's office. The mayor sent us to the Minister of Public Health. Brother Espinosa was accused of practicing medicine without a permit.

As we walked into the office, I said to the Minister of Public Health, "It was good to see you in my church the other night." He had attended a wedding in our church the week before. I told him that the evangelist used no medicines that, in fact, he did not even touch anyone when offering prayer for the sick and afflicted. I asked the minister if it was his practice to send an inspector to see firsthand whenever misconduct was reported. He replied in the affirmative, so I asked him to attend the service and to see for himself.

It did not end there. Brother Espinosa and I went back to the mayor's office, and there we were plainly told that the evangelist would no longer be allowed to speak in the services. I challenged the decision on the basis of the national constitution, which guaranteed freedom of religion. I also challenged the decision on the basis that the meetings were in the name of the Foursquare Church, which was duly registered with the government. From the mayor's office, our party was taken for a hearing before the Minister of Government and Justice. In the United States, the equivalent would be the Secretary of State. I was barred from attending, but later learned what had been said.

"We have no peace nor rest in our homes because of you," the Minister of Government and Justice told Evangelist Espinosa. "Certain religious leaders in the nation have influenced all our wives, even beginning with the wife of the president of the nation. We have no tranquility in our homes since you started the meetings. You have broken no laws, but please leave our country within three days." Since there was no other recourse, Brother Espinosa had to leave. I asked one of our missionaries to continue with the nightly services until the end of the month. God continued to heal people, and the newspapers reported, "Now we know it isn't the man that heals, but God."

I was urged to get the lot for more time, even though several of us knew it was best to end the campaign and urge the new converts to now begin attending churches of their choice. I went back to see the owner of the lot, ready to thank him for allowing us to use it. The moment I walked into his office, he and his staff told me the problems they had "suffered." He said, "Every day, all day long, our phones rang, with people asking us to get you off that lot. I told them over and over again that there was nothing I could do because you had my signed receipt granting use of the lot for one month." At that point, I was very thankful that I had insisted on paying for the use of the lot.

Two or three years later an amusing thing happened. We were ministering in our family camp for the Chiriquí Province near Jacú. One day at noon, I decided to get away for a little while by myself. Walking along a trail about a mile from camp, I met six civil engineers. They were working on plans for the Inter-American Highway that would be constructed through that area. One of them was the man that had let us use the lot for the crusade. He wanted to know if there was a restaurant in the area where they could get something to eat. I invited them to follow me, which they did, and I asked the camp cooks to feed them "real good." When the gentleman got out his wallet to pay for the six meals, I said, "No, it's on the camp. We may want to lease another one of your lots for a campaign sometime." To this he replied, "Oh please, no. I don't want to have to go through that again." We all had a good laugh.

In 1958 the Billy Graham crusade was held in Panama. Several months before the event, a meeting was held with representatives from twenty-seven church and parachurch organizations. I was asked to be the chairman of the crusade and was unanimously approved by all present. There were many meetings of the committee so that we could work out many details: prayer cells, advertising, ushers, preliminary meetings to train altar workers, and the various venues.

Before Dr. Graham arrived, crusades were held in the cities of David, Colon, and Panama City simultaneously, with members of the Billy Graham team as the speakers. Large crowds attended each service with good results. Dr. Graham arrived for the final four nights in the National Stadium in Panama City.

I had been asked by the organizing committee to arrange to use the stadium for the services, so I presented a formal written request to the national president, whom I had met a couple of times before. He said he would use his influence to grant us the stadium for the four nights. The decision really rested with the schedule of the Panama Baseball League. The vice president of the country was the chairman of that league and also an acquaintance of mine. One of his sons had been healed of paralysis in the Colon Foursquare Church.

Meanwhile, both political and ecclesiastical pressure from various groups mounted. Major newspapers said they would publish news about the meetings, but refused to advertise the crusade at the stadium. Carl Thompson, pastor of the Diablo Heights Foursquare/Canal Zone Church, printed tens of thousands of invitations and these were distributed all over the city.

The vice president had the unenviable task of trying to please all the factions. He called me and said that he would be absent during the crusade, attending a baseball series in Puerto Rico. He also said he was giving me his power of attorney. Should it have become necessary, I had the right to act on the vice president's behalf regarding the use of the stadium. Although it was not needed, I was thankful for the trust I was shown.

As if all the turmoil beforehand were not enough, all public transportation in the city went on strike for the four days of the services. But the people came and crowded out the stadium, and a very large number of people gave their hearts to the Lord.

Years later, I was walking along the main street in the center of Panama City. Traffic was stopped and backed up quite a distance. It was midday, very warm and humid, and tempers were flaring. As I walked, I wondered who in the world would be blocking the way. Finally, I approached the car that was holding everything up. At the wheel was the vice president of the country. He had seen me and stopped. He motioned for me to come over. He said, "Lilando, I have heard some sad news. I have learned that you are leaving my country." I replied in the affirmative and told him that we would be moving to Chile. He remarked, "That's bad news, but you can go away knowing that the Foursquare Church will continue to thrive and grow in my nation. You have taught my people the Word of God, so their conversations in their homes and with their neighbors center on Jesus and the gospel."

All of the crusades held during the 1950s added to the evangelical community, including the Foursquare Church. Those crusades are still bearing fruit in the kingdom to this time.

17

⊲ Going to the "Uttermost" Part

JESUS PROMISED HIS disciples that they would become wit-
nesses to the "uttermost" part of the earth. I am sure that He
saw the multitude of generations that would follow, as well
as the extreme places where His message would be proclaimed.
That would include the most remote villages and tribes of Panama, with their wide spectrum of culture, education, and living
styles. In addition, there was an urgency in the promise which, to
this day, presents us with the challenging question, "What about
those who never had the opportunity to hear the gospel?"

The Guaymi live in the mountain regions of the Chiriquí and
Bocas del Toro Provinces, bordering Costa Rica. The Guaymi
tribe is large, and, for the most part, the members stay in their
homeland. However, while we were in Panama, a few Guaymi
left home and found work on the banana plantation in southern
Costa Rica. They lived in the small company town of Coto 42,
one of the many company-owned villages in the banana zone in
Costa Rica, adjacent to Panama. The banana plantation, which
is still there, extends for many miles, all the way to the Pacific
Coast where large ships are loaded with fruit for the United
States and Europe.

Antonio Rojas, a lay-preacher from Panama, had established a
Foursquare church in the village of Coto 42. One of the converts
was Luisa Montesuma, a young Guaymi lady in her late teens or
early twenties. She had the desire to share her new life in Jesus
with her family back home. She journeyed into the mountains
of the Chiriquí Province of Panama and shared the gospel with
her family members for eight days. Twenty-six of them came to
the Lord. Realizing that these new believers would need to know

more about "the Way," Luisa went to Jacú, where Luis Harris lived. At that time, Luis was the supervisor of the Foursquare churches in the Chiriquí Province. She asked him to send a pastor to her people. He responded by making the trip up into the mountains to where these people lived, taking with him four of his church members. Greeting Luis upon his arrival were some 380 men, women, and children. Luis and his team stayed for one week, and each night at least fifty people gave their hearts to the Lord in the services. Luis appointed one of the men who had made the journey with him as pastor of the new congregation. This young pastor had a long trip to make each weekend, going to where these new Christians lived in the mountains to teach them the Word.

Several years have gone by since Luisa made the trip to give the gospel to her relatives. Since that time, the work has spread amongst the Guaymi, crossing the continental divide into the Atlantic side of the country. There are now thirty-one Foursquare Guaymi congregations in Panama, and the work has spread across the border to the Guaymi residing in Costa Rica. Members of the tribe now pastor almost all of these churches.

An uncle of Luisa, Francisco Montesuma, was one of the first people in the tribe to give his heart to the Lord. Francisco had three wives: Eva, Amalia, and Feliciana; they also received Jesus into their hearts. When Luis Harris learned that Francisco was a polygamist, he instructed the workers with him to ask the Lord for wisdom and timing regarding this matter. A year later, Eva told her husband that he and his wives were not living correctly. She had read in God's Word that a man is to have just one wife and that a woman is to have only one husband. Francisco initially replied that he would renounce his faith in Christ. The three ladies prayed for God's help. A few days later when they went to their church, he went along with them and asked God to help the four of them to do what was correct.

Francisco decided to just have one of them as his wife. He asked Eva to marry him, and she refused. Next, he asked Amalia, and she also refused. So a few days later he and Feliciana journeyed to Luis Harris' home in Jacú, with their marriage license, and Luis married them. Francisco divided his property and possessions with the three ladies. Then he and his wife, Feliciana, left their homeland up in the mountains of the Chiriquí Province and moved almost the length of the country, toward Colombia, where they settled in a small village named Piña. Today, he and his wife pastor the Foursquare Church there.

But there is more to the story about Eva. She became a leader in the church in Cerro Banco, in the very place where the work with the Guaymi had started. She helped in starting other congregations among her tribe. Once a month Luis Harris would go to Sabalo, a focal point for these churches, and conduct Bible classes with the church leaders, starting at eight thirty. Several people had to walk for many hours to attend. Eva and her group generally hiked on the trail for about five hours in the evening and, just short of their destination, would stop along the trail and sleep until daylight. The Guaymi women wear very colorful, long, flowing tribal dresses. On one occasion, a very poisonous viper crawled in under Eva's dress, probably seeking a warm place to sleep. When Eva awoke and moved her legs, the snake immediately bit her. Others of the group came to her rescue and killed the very poisonous snake. Eva's leg began to swell, but she walked the remaining distance in about an hour and asked Luis to pray for her. He did so but also told her that, according to Panamanian law, he was obligated to take her to the nearest hospital or clinic to receive an antivenin. Although her leg had swollen considerably, she refused, not wanting to miss the Bible class. About noon when the session was over, she again had Luis and all of the others pray for her, and she left to walk back home. Before reaching her house, she was completely healed. God had spared her life again, and Eva continues to minister to her tribe with a strong message of faith in Christ.

Decades later, the power of the gospel was experienced in another remote area of the nation. In the year 2000, in the

Rio San Pedro area in the Bocas del Toro Province of Panama, the leading brujo (witchdoctor) of the Guaymi in that region, came into the church, interrupting the worship and pronouncing his curse on all the people in attendance. He told them that the curse affected the paths they must take to get home and that they would be confused and unable to find their homes that night. The people left the service, but could not find their homes. They returned to the church. For the rest of the night, the pastor proclaimed a vigilia (watch-night service). These Guaymi sang and praised the Lord, proclaimed His Word, and prayed through that night and the next day, seeking victory over the power of the enemy. The witchdoctor returned to the church and said to them, "I said you would be confused and would not be able to find your dwelling places. Now, renounce your faith in Jesus or you will die." The people gathered around this evil man and began to plead the blood of Jesus against the demon that possessed him. They raised their hands to God as they prayed and asked for deliverance. Suddenly the brujo fell to the ground and died.

The news of this event spread. Within a few hours, the police had arrived on the scene and arrested all of those church members who had been present when the brujo dropped dead. They were charged for murder and were taken to the alcalde (mayor) of the district, the leading government authority. The case was heard, with each of the accused giving testimony of what had happened. The alcalde learned that no one had knocked the brujo down. In fact, no one had even touched him. The alcalde was so moved by the attitude and spirit of these Guaymi Christians that he ordered food brought in; they ate together while he learned more about the gospel. Many were far from home, and it would take them several hours in their dugout canoes to return to their region. The alcalde ordered fuel for their boats, which were powered by outboard motors, and they returned home rejoicing in the Lord.

During my years of working in Panama, we continued to take

the gospel to the outlying regions of the nation. A number of years ago, I made a trip to the Darien Province on the border with Colombia, a region regarded as the "frontier" of the nation. There were two ways to travel there, either by small coastal boats from Panama City or by light airplane to a very few dirt runways cleared from intense jungle growth. There were no roads for automobiles. All travel within the area was by boat on the rivers to the small towns built on their banks. Some of these small settlements were trading posts for the Choco Indian tribe, the original inhabitants. Over the years, especially during the last part of the nineteenth century and the first decades of the twentieth century, scores of people who were descendants of slaves in Colombia migrated to the Darien. Many of them lived there as illegal aliens, though their descendants later became citizens of Panama by birth.

One of the special towns in which I ministered was Chepigana, on the banks of the Tuira River. I stayed for three days, holding meetings with the leaders and members of the Foursquare church, teaching classes in the morning and conducting evangelistic services at night. Accompanying me on this trip was Dr. Fred Beard, a close friend who was also the supervisor of the Midwest District of Foursquare Churches in the United States. One afternoon we went out for a walk. Following a path through the jungle, we came to a small thatched hut on a hill overlooking the river.

As we approached, I saw an elderly member of the church sitting on a crude wooden stool in front of the door. He was reading his Bible. Because not many people of his age had learned to read, I asked him to read a portion of the Scripture. He slowly read from the Gospel of John where Jesus told His disciples that He was going away but that He would come again and receive them unto Himself so that they would be with Him eternally. After reading Jesus' words, "I am the way, and the truth, and the life; no one comes to the Father, but by me," he looked straight at me and posed a question that reflected the concern scholars have wrestled with for centuries. He said, "I am the second generation of my family to live here. My father and mother died. They never even had one chance to hear this message. They never heard about Jesus, the Savior. Are they lost? Did they go to be with Jesus?"

Like most people who know the Lord, I had asked myself that question more than once. However, knowing the background and circumstances of this case, I found it difficult to immediately reply. I could hardly hold back the tears. I could only say, "We know that God is just." How I wished I had a better answer. Fred and I sat there in silence for a short while. Then we joined hands and prayed together. Although we could not answer the question satisfactorily, we renewed our commitment to doing all we could to touch the world, to the "uttermost" part, with the good news of Jesus Christ.

18

◁ A Mighty Voice

FROM ANCIENT TIMES, the isthmus of Panama has been a center of trade and communication. All tribal people going north or south in the Americas had to travel on trails that passed through what is now Panama. With the opening of the Panama Canal Panama became known as the "Crossroads of the World." It was to that crossroads that my parents took the message of the Foursquare gospel, and it has been proclaimed with a mighty voice to Panama and all its neighbors. The gospel has been heard in the halls of government and in the homes of the average citizen. And in both of those settings, it has been received with great rejoicing.

Presidents and dictators need the gospel just as "normal" people do. One morning I walked into the Santo Tomas Hospital in Panama City to visit one of our church members. The president of Panama, who was also a medical doctor, passed by on his way out. Down the hallway, I met the head nurse for that ward. Since she was a member of our church, I asked her if it was Dr. Arias, the president, who had just left the hospital, and if she knew him. She told me that it was indeed the president and that he was a good friend of hers. I then told her that, if she ever had the opportunity to do so, I wanted her to tell the president that "El Gringo Lilando" (my name in some government circles) would like to meet him. I had just gotten back to our home when the phone rang. She said, "I called the president and he said he would like you to come to his house this afternoon at two o'clock."

Several years before, when Dr. Arias was in his first term as president of Panama, persecution arose against the Foursquare

Church as well as all Protestant and Evangelical churches. The government closed all of our churches with the exception of those in Panama City and Colon. Dad, along with other church leaders, secured the help of lawyers; that action resulted in the Panama Supreme Court declaring that the national constitution guarantees religious liberty. Our churches and others were all reopened within a couple of months.

Before his first term was over, the president was ousted through a short revolution and lived in exile for several years. Finally, he was allowed to return to his country; after several years he was nominated by a local political party to run for president in the next election. About that time, one of our regular radio listeners came to our home asking us to secure for him the very finest Spanish Bible in print, which we did. I asked him what he was going to do with it, and he said that it was a present for Dr. Arias. I said, "Do me a favor. Ask him if, should he be successful in the elections, he will close the churches again." A few days later I received word from this man that, while he was in exile, Dr. Arias had learned that the gospel in Panama had really helped the Panamanian people. Dr. Arias also asked who had asked that question. My friend replied, "El Gringo Lilando."

I was hoping that the president remembered those events as clearly as I did, but I was still a bit nervous when the two o'clock appointment rolled around. I took Claude Updike with me, and we were very cordially received in the president's home. He gave us all the time we wanted. We had a good conversation with him about the Lord, sharing how He loves us and what He did so that we can experience His love. We asked him if he would like to give his heart to the Lord, to which he replied in the affirmative. He then repeated a prayer asking the Lord to be his Savior. We finished the interview by asking the Lord to help him in his administrative responsibilities.

Later, well into his term in office, there was another revolution to try to topple the government. One afternoon, our head nurse came hurrying to the church office and said, "Your friend is in deep trouble and needs to see you." I told her she should go with us. As we approached the area of the president's office, there seemed to be a lull in the shooting. We drove to our destination displaying the Red Cross flag out the window. Again we had prayer with Dr. Arias, and I read to him from my Bible some verses that were meaningful for the occasion. He wanted my Bible, so I left it with him. As we began to drive away, again we could hear machine-gun fire. He was overthrown and was granted asylum in the United States.

There were three other times I went to see a president of Panama. When planning for the Billy Graham crusade, I went to talk to the president about the use of the national stadium for the meetings. As chairman of the crusade, I had the privilege of going with the U. S. ambassador when he took Dr. Graham to talk with the president. I served as Dr. Graham's interpreter for that occasion.

One very significant meeting was with the very famous Juan Domingo Peron, former dictator of Argentina, who had spent many months in exile in Panama. He is probably best remembered as the husband of Evita Peron. One day a friend visiting from the United States asked me if I would get an appointment to see the dictator. I did that through my friend, Jose Bazan, who was the mayor of the city of Colon. Mr. Bazan's son had been healed of paralysis in a meeting in our Colon church. At the time, Mr. Peron was living in the Washington Hotel in that city. He was very lenient with his time. We talked for at least an hour and a half. He was a socialist, politically, and knew many portions of the Bible by memory, especially any sayings of Jesus that he could use for his socialistic doctrines. When I asked him if he would like to know the Lord as his Savior, he knelt with us and repeated the sinner's prayer.

A year later, I felt the Lord wanted me to see Mr. Peron again. This time he was living in a private house. Again, I got permission to see him through the same mayor of Colon. That was necessary to get past the guard. This time, however, the guard was not going to grant entrance. I was turning away when Mr. Peron saw me through the window and signaled to the guard to let me in. I wanted to talk to him about really being a dedicated Christian. We began with a friendly visit. He had the ability to make people feel right at home. I read the first chapter of the First Epistle of John to him, emphasizing, "If we walk in the light as He is in the light, we have fellowship with one another, and the blood of Jesus Christ His Son cleanses us from all sin." And if we sin, "We have an advocate with the Father, Jesus Christ the Righteous." We talked about living for Jesus, living a life that is acceptable unto God. Soon afterward he left the country, and I do not know what he did with the Word. But the gospel seed had been sown in those interviews. These were some of the fulfilling experiences I will never forget.

Another very fulfilling ministry for a missionary is to "make disciples of all nations...teaching them to observe all things that I have commanded you." Yet, in making disciples, we faced quite a challenge in discovering practical ways. We had three Bible institutes functioning in the three largest cities of the nation, but Panama was a country with a large rural population. Many of our church members and potential leaders lived on their small farms, and their family roots were deep. To come into the city to enroll in the institute while maintaining their livelihood would have been impossible for many. They still had their families to support. Besides, we needed more pastors and teachers who knew the rural life. So we decided to take the Bible studies to them. Applicants registered with the leadership in each province, and teachers from our city institutes volunteered, along with Barb and me, to conduct classes in provincial centers. Generally the classes averaged three days and nights at intervals of two months. This method was slow, but it produced fruitful, effective workers for the Lord.

Covering the entire nation of Panama and beyond had always been the goal of the Panama Church. After Aimee Semple McPherson visited Panama in 1939 and preached in some of the

Foursquare churches, she had the vision of putting a powerful radio station in that country. Virtually every home and every saloon had a radio receiver. It was the common practice of most of the people to turn the radio on as soon as they arose and leave it on all day. In the very early 1940s, Barbara and I began broadcasting the gospel over longwave and shortwave commercial stations, using local talent.

The ministry that we started so many decades ago is still producing. In 1998 Ilya Carrera had a God-given vision to enter radio ministry. She was backed by the Foursquare congregation she pastored in Bethania, a section of greater Panama City. She rented a local station and became its manager; members of the church staffed it. Previously, she had a radio and television ministry on local commercial stations.

Ilya's mother, Telma, had been saved under the ministry of my parents in the Panama City church. She later went to Los Angeles, California, studied at LIFE Bible College, and graduated four years later. Returning to Panama, she married a young man she met in the church. From childhood their daughter, Ilya, became active in church work; she graduated from the Arthur Edwards Bible Institute and pioneered the Bethania Foursquare Church. A very gifted church leader, Ilya Carrera has served as a member of the board of directors of the Panama Foursquare Church, as a Bible institute instructor, as president of the Panama Ministerial Alliance, and as a director of the Panama Bible Society. She often accepts invitations to minister in other countries.

In November 1998, Foursquare President and Mrs. Paul Risser visited Panama. As Ilya drove them around the city, she told them the vision the Lord had given her regarding expanding the radio ministry in Panama. Dr. Risser invited her to attend the International Foursquare Convention to be held in Dallas in the spring of 1999. She was allotted fifteen minutes to explain what God had laid on her heart. At that time there was a radio station for sale in Panama, and she asked the people to pray.

At the convention Dr. Risser invited Ilya to the platform

because they had a surprise for her. Doctor Rolf McPherson, son of Aimee Semple McPherson, told the convention body how his mother had had a vision and even raised and put aside money to put a strong station in Panama. However, World War II prevented the fulfillment of that vision. Dr. McPherson stated that the Foursquare Church would help fund a radio station in Panama.

Upon her return to Panama, Ilya went right to work. The station that had been for sale was withdrawn from the market. She decided to seek a license for a new station, one that would have four frequencies, with repeater stations in three other locations of the nation. The Panamanian government was going through some changes affecting communications. But God answered prayer. In 2001, Radio Voz Poderosa (Radio Mighty Voice) went on the air. Dr. McPherson had recalled that, when KFSG was dedicated in 1924 at Angelus Temple, the station went on the air with the song "Give the Winds a Mighty Voice." He suggested the name for the Panama Foursquare Radio: Mighty Voice. The people in Panama liked it, and the station logo still bears the name: Radio Voz Poderosa.

The studio is adjacent to the auditorium of the Bethania Foursquare Church, and its tower is on top of the highest mountain some twenty miles away. From there its signal is beamed out to repeater stations. The Foursquare message is now heard throughout the whole country and into neighboring Colombia and Costa Rica. The Mighty Voice radio station is a fully automated facility and is on the air twenty-four hours daily. Many of the transmissions are live. Services are broadcast from the Bethania Foursquare Church; there are programs for the youth by the youth; there are programs for the children; and there is also a talk-show counseling program. Many souls are receiving Christ through the radio ministry that includes such varied programming.

In March 2001, Barbara and I were privileged to minister in Panama. One of the highlights of that trip was preaching in the

Bethania church, a large thriving congregation. I preached in the two Sunday morning services, the first of which was broadcast live. We rejoiced in the fulfillment of the vision of our church's founder, Aimee Semple McPherson. Her vision of giving the airwaves a "mighty voice" was almost a century old. It had now been realized through another anointed lady, Ilya Carrera.

19

◁ Barb's Special Memories

ABOUT ONE HUNDRED miles from Panama City there is a small settlement called Pajonal. To get there we had to travel via car to the town of Penonomé. Leaving our car, we would walk some five hours over mountains, crossing rivers five different times. We traveled the trails at night because it was cooler.

I remember one time that, upon our arrival at midnight, the little adobe church was packed with people waiting for us. Many of these people had walked nine hours to get there. They were hungry for the Word to be preached, so we began service at midnight. The benches were logs cut in half; they had no backs and were not very comfortable. But the meeting time and the seating were not the only things different from those in American churches.

Pajonal mothers wove hammock-type bags that they used to carry their babies. Once the babies were placed in the "carry-ons," the sling-type hammocks were placed on the mothers' foreheads, and the babies were carried on the mothers' backs. For many hours, even as many as nine, the Pajonal women could walk with the babies in the "strollers" on their backs! The one-room church building in Pajonal had pegs around the walls, so often babies were hung on the walls on those pegs. If, during the service, the babies cried, the mothers simply got up, went over, and patted their little bottoms until the babies quieted down. That was the "nursery," Pajonal style!

GOD'S PROTECTION

I remember another trip to the little settlement of Pajonal in the interior of Panama. Pajonal is up in the mountains in a very beautiful area. Hermano Tiburcio pastored the church, and each Saturday evening he and two of his helpers would meet to pray for the coming Sunday services. Because the people walked many hours one way, a one-hour service just wouldn't do!

As Hermano Tiburcio and his helpers met to pray in a little one-room adobe house with no windows or back door, they heard a commotion outside. Three drunken men with machetes came walking up the path. They were yelling, "We know you evangelicals are in there! We heard you praying. We are going to kill you."

There was no way that Hermano Tiburcio and the other two men could leave the one-room house. So they separated, one in one corner, another in another, with Hermano Tiburcio in the middle. The drunken attackers broke down the door, staggering around and cursing, saying that they knew the brothers were there. But they were never able to find the pastor and his helpers. Finally, they left. Later Hermano Tiburcio told Leland they were in that room but God had blinded the eyes of those evil men.

A PANAMA CHRISTMAS STORY

Emilia was a pretty nine-year-old girl. One March she attended vacation Bible school at the Avenida A Foursquare Church in Panama City. She was such a happy little girl and had a marvelous experience with Jesus. After the VBS, she continued attending the services, and she grew in the Lord.

Christmas Eve is always a big night in the churches in Panama. "Noche Buena!" is heard everywhere. In the Foursquare church, the children would have the first part of the service, with many recitations and short dramas. There would then be an intermission, after which the youth would present a Christmas drama. At midnight, everyone left church to go home and celebrate the birth of Jesus with family and friends, enjoying homemade tamales and other goodies.

That Christmas, just before service, Emilia's Sunday school teacher brought her to me. I had never seen the little girl sad, but this night she wasn't the bubbly little girl I knew. Her teacher said, "Show Hermana Barbarita your arms." Emilia had on a pretty sleeveless dress. Her arms had been scratched and pinched, obviously done with someone's fingernails. When I asked her what happened, she tearfully admitted that her mother had done it. She explained, "She didn't want me to come tonight. She thought I would be ashamed to come with my arms so bruised. But I couldn't stay away. This is Christmas Eve and we are celebrating the birth of Jesus." Then she uttered these profound words, "But this wasn't really my mother that did this. She just doesn't know Jesus. And when she does, she will be sorry that she did this!"

We are not sure whether the mother ever came to find Christ. However, like many other children around the world, this little girl had learned that it costs to be a witness for Jesus. And she had no regrets—she realized that living for Jesus is worth whatever it costs.

A New Name Written in Glory

About eighteen miles from Panama City there is an area called Chilibre, where most of the people live on small farms. They grow plantain, bananas, oranges, and grapefruit. The church was set back off the road. I drove out there one Sunday morning for service. Upon my arrival, the people said that an elderly man who lived behind the church (a short walk away) was sick and wanted to see me.

After the meeting I went with several of the members. It seems his family was very opposed to the gospel and did not want to have anything to do with us. But, because he was insistent, they permitted it. I had the blessed experience of leading him to the Lord while his family was gathered there.

Several weeks later I returned again to Chilibre, and I asked about the elderly man. The members were smiling. They remembered, "He passed away several days afterward. As he was dying he lifted his eyes and with a beautiful smile on his face said, 'Oh, don't you see them? They are dressed in white and they are coming for me!'" With those words he crossed over into the beautiful Heavenly City. He would experience no more pain, suffering, or sadness. All is joy and peace. For this dear newly converted brother, "eternity had just begun."

THE BIBLE—THE WRITTEN WORD

Deep in the interior of Panama is the village of Jaguito. We were holding a week of intense Bible teaching for pastors who had families and were farmers. It was not possible for them to come to the city for training, so we would take the "training" to them. We also published a monthly paper with helps and articles. The particular issue we were working on at the time featured the importance of the "family altar." It told of the necessity of gathering the family together for prayer and reading the Word.

Hermana Cuca was a beautiful little lady about seventy years old. She was dressed in the typical interior dress (long skirt with a loose white top), and her white hair hung in two long braids down her back. We knew she was the one for the front-page photo. A little table with a kerosene lamp and the open Bible were the "props." She sat down and, all of a sudden, she placed her bowed head on the Bible and started to weep. I put my arm around her and asked if we had done something to offend her. "No, Sister Barbarita. I am crying because this is La Palabra de Dios (the Word of God) and I cannot read it!" She continued to say that God had been so good to her. He had saved her, healed her, and her entire family had come to know the Lord. Then I remembered that the Bible is a "live book," the living Word. She couldn't read, but through God's minister who gave her the message, the Holy Spirit whispered to her heart that this was the truth.

That's not all—her story continues. Nearly twenty years later, I was once again in Jaguito for a youth camp. Leland and I had returned to the United States several years earlier, and he was the director of Foursquare Missions at this time. I asked the pastor about this little lady. "Oh, yes, you mean Hermana Cuca. She is the oldest person in the village. She is over ninety years old and blind." I wanted to go see her, so I arranged to make that visit with our son Loren, who was then a missionary in Panama. When Loren and I entered Hermana Cuca's little room, there she was, now blind, sitting up in bed. I greeted her, telling her who I was. When I included Leland's name in telling her who I was, she smiled and asked how the children were. Well, the boys were now married and had children of their own. But, I told her they were fine. We served communion to her. And then this beautiful little, wrinkled ninety-year-old turned her face my way and said: "All these years I have lived for Jesus. He has never failed me. I love Him. You are going back to the United States, and I will never see you again." Then she lifted one arm toward heaven and said, "But I will see you up there."

I was reminded that day of why Leland and I had spent our lives telling the story of Jesus. It is because it makes it possible for us to see so many people "up there."

20

◄ Fulfillment of the Call

F ROM THE BEGINNING of the Foursquare Church in Panama in 1928, my family had kept its residence in Panama City and often worked from there in ministry to other parts of the nation. The Central Church in Panama City became a beehive of activity; all of us were busy in ministry. The church in Panama City was also the main training center for national ministers and workers. Dad was the supervisor of the Foursquare Church in the nation and, along with Mother, pastored the Headquarters Church.

Donald and his wife, Edith, were very much involved in ministry in Panama City and nearby young churches. In 1937 they moved across the isthmus to Colon, the second largest city in the nation, to pastor the Colon church and direct the extending work in the Colon Province. In 1947 they felt called of the Lord to leave Panama, and, after a brief time in Guatemala, Don was appointed supervisor of the Foursquare Church in the West Indies. Don and Edith lived first in Ponce, Puerto Rico, and later in Havana, Cuba.

I entered into full-time ministry in June of 1937. I became the leader of the youth—the Foursquare Crusaders, as they were then called—in the Headquarters Church and, eventually, for the nation. I was young, still in my late teens, and I frequently traveled throughout the country ministering in the churches. After our marriage in August of 1941, Barbara and I continued in that ministry.

A few years later, Dad and Mother felt led of the Lord to resign as pastors of the Central Church. They turned this responsibility over to Barb and me. Dad continued as the supervisor of the field. But the time came when he said, "I'm getting along in years and I want to retire before the people remember me for what I was instead of for what I am." In August 1947, after nineteen years of missionary ministry in Panama, my parents decided that the time had come for them to retire. They returned to the United States to live on the ranch near Morgan Hill, California.

Barb and I lived in a small, rented, two-bedroom house in a suburb of Panama City called San Francisco. The house was built on poles about eight feet above the ground, with metal screening all the way around in place of glass windows. It was a style that was very popular at the time. We were living there when our first child, Arthur Noyes Edwards, was born in June 1943. Later we moved into the old frame quarters of the Central Church in Panama City. Our second son, Loren Jonathan Edwards, was born in February 1947.

After I had begun full-time ministry, I asked the Lord to give me a wife who played the piano and especially the accordion. In Barb, God answered that prayer. Her ability in music became a real asset to us in our ministry. Being adjacent to the church and the office, our home was easily accessible to members of our churches, especially young people. It was where we would have get-togethers with our missionaries. On Christmas, Thanksgiving, and the Fourth of July our missionaries in Panama would come to our home for a good meal and a time of fun.

There were also times during the course of the year when our missionary family would come together for times of fasting and prayer as well as for planning and fellowship. At times one of our fellow missionaries would need special prayer for healing. For instance, Lucille Hicks, one of our lady missionaries, was facing serious surgery. We gathered to read the Word, fast, and pray. We started in the morning, and around two o'clock we knew for sure that God had healed her. The next day she returned to the doctor. He examined her and said, "It is nothing I have done, but a miracle has taken place. You are well!" We continued these missionary fellowships through all the years of our time spent in Panama.

The four of us—Art, Loren, Barb, and I—did things together as a family. On Saturdays we generally would leave our home and go to a swimming hole along the river. We would have breakfast and then lunch and stay until late in the afternoon; it was our way of getting away from the phone and any visitors. When our boys played Little League Baseball, we took time to watch them. We kept busy for the Lord in ministry, but also in ministry to our family. We met together for devotions each day and attended our church services as a family. Before our sons started school and then during school vacations, they traveled with us on trips to hold services in different parts of the nation, including the five summer camps we conducted each year.

During World War II most of the country of Panama, including the Canal Zone, was blacked out. Homes and public buildings had to have the windows covered so that the light would not reflect out into the streets. Headlights on cars were covered with black paint with a slit below the center of the lens, two inches long and one inch wide, which cut down considerably on the brightness of the lights. We were allowed only four gallons of gasoline a week per car. To replace worn out tires, we would purchase another used car with good tires; we would then put the good tires on our car and the worn out ones on the newly purchased vehicle and then resell it.

During World War II, Panama became a major training ground for jungle warfare, preparing U. S. servicemen for battle in the Pacific. I was chairman of the Isthmian Religious Federation, composed mostly of clergy from the Canal Zone and chaplains of the U. S. Military in the Canal Zone and Panama. We became acquainted with many chaplains; some were invited over those years to speak in our Panama City Church. We were also invited to visit training camps. Barb would conduct sing-alongs, using her accordion. The troops really enjoyed having us serve them in that way. After the war, the large airbase in Rio

Hato, Panama, about sixty miles from our home, was without a Protestant chaplain for about three months. The head chaplain of the U. S. Caribbean Defense Command invited us to fill that vacancy on Sunday mornings until a new chaplain was assigned. I accepted his invitation, and each Sunday morning I drove to Albrook Field, where I would be flown in an Air Force plane to Rio Hato and back after the service. The first Sunday, the base chapel was only one-third filled. Soon, it became known that the gospel was being preached at the base. It wasn't long before the chapel on Sunday morning was packed. I felt very honored and thankful for the opportunity to minister to our servicemen. This was an unexpected but very satisfying part of my fulfilling God's call on my life.

When Dad and Mother retired, the international board in Los Angeles appointed me to serve as supervisor of the Panama field, a position I held until the end of 1959. God gave us favor and acceptance by our churches and with many authorities in the government. Barb and I both preached several times a week in the Headquarters Church as well as in our churches in outlying areas; we also taught several hours weekly in our Bible institute. Our radio broadcasts were done live, and we frequently made trips to visit the work in the interior of the country. We were very busy, but we loved it.

Even with the shortage of many materials during the war, we enlarged the auditorium of the Central Church to twice its original size. Because of the amazing growth, it was still filled to capacity, especially on Sunday nights for the evangelistic services. Very often we preached illustrated sermons, using members of the church in live scenes. I designed and made props for scenery for the platform, and our people enjoyed taking part. In the mid-1950s, we again enlarged the main auditorium of the Central Church. This time, we added space for offices and rooms that doubled for Sunday school and the Bible institute.

The annual national convention was held each year in November in the Panama City Foursquare Church. Pastors and delegates came by bus from all over the nation and from across the border in southern Costa Rica, where several churches had been pioneered through the ministry of Antonio Rojas, one of our national pastors in the Chiriquí Province. From the Darien Province, bordering with Colombia, they came by small coastal boats. The delegates slept in the homes of our members, and many slept on the benches of the church after the evening services. Convention was a great time of fellowship. In the dry season the first three months of the year, camps were held in five different areas of the country. We loved every opportunity to be with the church members in every part of the nation.

TWO SIGNIFICANT EVENTS

In God's wise mercy, there comes a time in a person's life when an event or series of events occur, releasing a new season of ministry. In my case, the first was the passing of my father, literally fulfilling his vision to the fullest. I firmly believe that, at that moment, a new phase of my own calling was launched.

It was June 1955. Barb and I and our two sons, Arthur and Loren, were on furlough from Panama and speaking in churches in the northwestern section of the United States. I was on the platform of the Portland, Oregon, Foursquare Church to speak in the service that night during the Northwest District convention. The auditorium was completely filled. Most of those in attendance were ministers from all over that portion of the country. When Dr. Mourer, supervisor of the district, finished introducing me, he handed me a telegram as I walked to the pulpit. Without opening it, I put it in my coat pocket and delivered the message for that evening. When I returned to my chair, I remembered the telegram. I opened it and read these words from my mother: "Your father is very ill. Please return home. We need you." I took the telegram to Dr. Mourer, and he had the convention body stand and earnestly pray for Dad. Before going to bed that night I called my mother in Morgan Hill, California.

She told me that God had touched Dad and that he wanted us to continue our itinerary. We traveled for one week, speaking in Vancouver, British Columbia, and eastern Washington. Mother sent another telegram asking us to return home, which we did, arriving there on July 5.

The next day I took Dad to the doctor. His condition was very serious: he had a tumor the size of a grapefruit in his bladder. As we were taking him to the hospital in Gilroy, California, he made us promise not to consent to surgery. The doctor had said that, considering his overall physical condition, he would have a fifty-fifty chance of living through surgery. If he did make it, he would be confined to a wheelchair for the rest of his life. He was seventy-four years old. God had given him and Mother outstanding ministries over many years, and it seemed his strength was spent.

I wanted to know what God was going to do with my father, so I told the Lord I would fast and pray up to fourteen days to seek His answer. My parents lived out of town on a prune and walnut orchard. A short distance from the house was a small cabin, now empty, where Grandpa Edwards had lived during his final years. Barb agreed to my plan to fast and pray, so I locked myself in that cabin and began my time of fasting and prayer with the Lord. On the fourth day, God in His own special way told me: *I am going to take your father "home" to be with Me on the twenty-eighth of this month [July].* I didn't ask Him for a fleece, but He gave me two: *So that you will know this is true, you will receive two letters in the mail tomorrow.* The Lord gave me word for word the content of each letter. I told Barb what the Lord had said. The next day those two letters came in the mail, exactly as God had told me. Daily we went to the hospital to spend time with Dad, taking Mother with us. All of the family agreed that we must honor Dad's request and not subject him to surgery. Late in the night of July twenty-eighth, Dad left for heaven. His body was laid to rest in the cemetery in Morgan Hill.

The way God ministered to me that day, while in communion with Him, has to be one of the greatest experiences of my life. Why? Because with all of the vast population of this earth, God proved to me that He has time to come and minister to just one person. Furthermore, God confirmed that His plan for my future was just as carefully designed as had been the details surrounding the death of my father.

God gives a call for ministry, but He also has His timing for it to take place. Many people receive what they believe is a call from God, but do not wait for the opening of God's door to fulfill that special ministry. I was about to make that mistake in my own life. In fact, that near mistake is what brought about the second significant event I experienced, which occurred after Barb and I had been pastors of the Headquarters Church in Panama for several years. In the twelve months preceding that event, over 350 people had found Christ at the altar of the church. Many had been baptized in water, a good number had been baptized with the Holy Spirit, miracles of healing had taken place, and the church was overflowing with people. Our radio broadcasts were popular and reaching many people. I was supervisor of the entire Panama field, which then numbered over 150 churches. Bible institutes had been established in key cities of Panama. But I got the idea that I would like to be an international evangelist. So, I promised God that I would fast and pray up to fourteen days to seek His answer, which I hoped would be approval for my plans.

In the late afternoon of the fourteenth day, the heavens were still brass, and there had been no answer from God. Finally I broke down and began to cry. I said to the Lord, "I dedicated fourteen days of fasting and prayer and You are silent. I get no answer from You." God replied in His own special way: All this time you have been telling Me what you want to do and how you want to do it. Be still and listen. I will tell you what My will is. Have I not been blessing you and using you right here in Panama? I don't need you as an international evangelist. I have many that are fulfilling that ministry. If you continue to be faithful where you are and in the responsibilities that I have given you, including supervision of the Panama field, I will eventually make your horizons unlimited.

I knew God had answered. I broke out in thanksgiving and praises unto Him. It was a time I will never forget. I immediately dismissed the idea of changing ministries; He gave me a renewed desire to stay where He had us, and I put my whole heart and soul into what God had us doing. And it was years later that I came to understand what God meant by "unlimited horizons."

21

◄ The Faith Promise

DURING OUR FURLOUGH in the United States in 1955, we attended the annual missionary conference in Angelus Temple. The conference speaker was Dr. Oswald J. Smith from Toronto, Canada. Each night, before his evening message on missions, he explained what he called the "faith promise."

The meetings were nightly for a whole week, and on the final Sunday the ingathering took place. Each person received an envelope on which were printed these words: "Trusting God to help me, I will endeavor to give _____ dollars per month to Foursquare Missions." Spaces were provided to check off a dollar amount and a line for the name of the contributor. It was a "faith promise" and not a pledge. If the Lord didn't supply the funds, the person did not have to pay the amount promised. The faith promise was over and above the tithe and regular offerings to the church. The donors were also promised that they would never receive a request or be dunned for their promises.

In each service Dr. Smith gave testimonies about people that had made faith promises and how God had supplied them with unexpected funds so they could fulfill their commitments. He related what the Lord did for them spiritually as well as financially. We attended the service each evening and I said, "This method will work any place in the world, even amongst the poorest saints."

Back in Panama from that furlough, we conducted a missionary conference in the Central Church. Dad, the founder of the Foursquare Church in Panama, had passed away that year, and we called it a memorial missionary conference. Dad had always stressed missions, believing that the Panamanian believers would take the gospel to their own nation and to countries beyond. I asked Rev. Patricio Rodriguez to be the conference speaker. He was a man who had been saved under Dad's ministry and had left a very fine position with the Panama Canal Company to go to the interior of Panama to preach the gospel.

My! What a time we had. We had set a goal for a large sum—especially large for the economy of that country. As the faith promises were gathered, the indicator on the "thermometer" on the platform rose higher and higher. It rose much higher than our goal, and the whole church stood and sang the chorus, "Alleluia."

Did the faith promises come in? Yes they did! We had had a missionary program going for several years, sending laborers out into the field, and this really gave it a big push. The program was soon being used in several of our Panama churches.

God blessed those that participated. Of the many testimonies of how God gave the people over and above what they had promised, I will tell about Diana. During the collection of the faith promises, she came to the edge of the platform wanting to talk to me. She said, "You know about me. My parents died and my oldest brother gets odd jobs to take care of me and my brothers and sisters. I finished my courses in a business school, and I have been walking the streets for days trying to find work and it looks almost hopeless. Tell me, what should I promise the Lord?" I told her to go back to her seat and talk to the Lord and then put down the amount she could believe Him for on her faith promise card. The next day after the conference, I looked through the faith promise cards and found one with Diana's name on it. She had made a promise of several dollars a month. I knew she was the poorest of the poor. Prior to the midweek service, she came early to see me. Something wonderful had happened; I could tell by the smile on her face. She said, "Today I was hired in the accounting department of the city hospital—not the lowest position, but well up the ladder. I will be able to give what I promised monthly, well ahead of schedule with the salary I will receive." And she did.

Many of our churches in the nation began to hold missionary conferences, using the faith promise method. And guess what—in all of them the tithes and offerings increased also. Barb and I continued to be blessed in this ministry of missionary conferences over many years and in many countries, including the United States.

22

⊲Celebrating God's Faithfulness

FORTY-FIVE YEARS HAVE come and gone since my family and I left Panama as resident missionaries. From Panama, Barbara and I relocated to Chile where we served for a year bringing healing to a group of fifty churches spread out across the length of that nation. I served as supervisor of the work in Chile and the works in Argentina and Panama. Because our furlough would be due at the end of 1959, Barb took our two sons to Glendale, California, to attend public school. The boys stayed with Barbara's parents while we returned to Chile.

At the end of our time in Chile, Barb left by a freight ship and picked up our small amount of personal belongings in Panama. Then we went on to Los Angeles to begin furlough. Both of us enjoyed traveling by ship, especially freighters. We reunited with our sons and were able to celebrate Christmas that year as a family.

When the missionary cabinet of the U.S. Foursquare Church held its annual meetings in February 1960, I was asked by Dr. McPherson, who was president of the denomination at that time, to join the staff of the Foreign Missions Department as assistant to the director, Dr. Herman D. Mitzner. My wife was also asked to work in the office as part of the secretarial staff and as the manager of the missionary furlough home near Angelus Temple. For the next five years, I made ministry trips to speak in conventions and conferences, as well as local churches in most of Latin America, the Far East, and the South Pacific. Some of the trips lasted more than two months, and in some of the countries I was asked to deal with local and field problems. On each field, I stayed in the homes of our missionaries, thereby becoming closely acquainted with them and their families.

During the 1965 International Foursquare Convention in Moline, Illinois, I was installed as the director of Foreign Missions (later the name "Foreign Missions" was changed to Foursquare Missions International). I became a member of the board of directors of the Foursquare Church. After our sons completed their high school years, the door opened for Barbara to travel with me on most of my overseas ministry visits. Our missionaries were very happy for her fellowship, her input for their lives, and her teaching and preaching.

In 1988 we retired from the office and moved to Lancaster, California, where we now live. During the twenty-three years I served as director of the missions program, the number of countries in which Foursquare ministered increased from twenty-seven to seventy-four. From our home in the high desert of Southern California, we have been used by the Lord to encourage pastors and church leaders. From time to time we are invited to minister outside the United States in conventions and conferences.

Our children have also been blessed. Our older son, Arthur, has taught Spanish and French in high school for over thirty-nine years. He and his wife, Beverly, are very active in church work. Our other son, Loren, and his wife, Cheilon, served as missionaries in Venezuela and Panama. They presently pastor the La Mision del Rey Foursquare Church in North Hills, California. The Lord has blessed us with five married grandchildren and ten great-grandchildren; all of them are attending Foursquare churches.

As we look back, we see how the Lord has been faithful to His promise:

> And every one who has left houses or brothers or sisters or
> father or mother or children or lands, for my name's sake,
> will receive a hundredfold, and inherit eternal life.
> —MATTHEW 19:29

We have never been sorry that we said yes to the call of the Lord. It has been a great privilege to be missionaries and to minister to precious brothers and sisters around the world.

There is also another area of fulfillment. In January 2003 my wife and I traveled to Panama to participate in the diamond anniversary of the Foursquare Church in that nation. Pastors and members assembled from all over the country to attend the evening services in the El Panama Convention Center. Daily seminars were conducted in the national headquarters and Bible college building. Several former missionaries, including my brother Donald and two of his daughters, enjoyed the festivities.

On the final afternoon of the convention, an estimated ten thousand Foursquare members marched in a parade. Beginning at the Legislative Plaza in the center of Panama City, men and women, boys and girls marched for five miles, waving their Panamanian and Foursquare flags, regional banners, balloons, distributing tracts, and singing en route to the stadium where the final service was to be held. There are now more than four hundred Foursquare churches and one hundred-fifty meeting places (many of which will become churches) spread the length and breadth of Panama.

Barb and I watched with tears in our eyes as the thousands of Foursquare members assembled for the celebration. Many were fourth generation Foursquare people, including babies we had dedicated who were grown and many who had trained under our leadership and were now strong ministers preaching and teaching the Word of God. Years before, God promised that He would make my horizons unlimited if I remained obedient to Him. He had been faithful to fulfill that promise. Barb and I felt blessed to have had a part in this beautiful work of God's grace on a nation.

It all began because a couple in northern California was willing to leave their home and take their family to Panama in obedience to the call of God on their lives. Seventy-five years ago, my father and mother shed tears as they anticipated the harvest. Now, Barb and I shed tears of joy as we look back on the harvest that has occurred and look ahead to an even greater harvest to come. Tens of thousands will enter heaven because two faithful followers of Jesus Christ—filled with His Spirit—dared to "chase the vision."

Appendix A
◁ Missionaries Who Have Served in Panama

THE PARAGRAPH UNDER each name is just a small resumé. Some of the activities of each party are listed. Many pages could be written about each one and what was done for the Lord. Yet, for these memoirs, I am including only those who served in Panama from 1928 through 1959, during the time I was in Panama.

Arthur and Edith Edwards arrived in Panama February 1, 1928, accompanied by their children: Donald, Barbara, and Leland. They started the Foursquare Church in the Republic of Panama. They had no pre-arrival contacts for ministry with any personnel in the country, and they started their ministry in a secondhand tent that was erected on a rented lot in Panama City. Throughout the following years, the work spread over the length and breadth of the country. Dr. Edwards had the Foursquare Church officially registered with the national government and constructed the first church buildings. He served as the first supervisor of the church until their departure in August 1947. Arthur died in 1955, and Edith in 1968.

Donald and Edith Edwards served together in Panama for more than ten years. Donald was in his late teens when he arrived in Panama and began helping in the work, playing his trombone, and preaching in the services. He occasionally worked for the Panama Canal and was appointed a Foursquare missionary in 1934. Edith worked for the Panama Canal. Donald and Edith were married in Gatun, Canal Zone, in 1935. They ministered in Panama City and surrounding areas, also teaching in the Bible institute. Later they moved to Colon and were pastors of the church in that city for several years, opening churches on the

Caribbean coast. They left Panama in 1947 and served in Puerto Rico and later in Cuba, supervising the Foursquare Church in the West Indies until 1960. They were also missionaries in Bolivia from 1967 to 1968. Donald lives in Scotts Valley, California; Edith passed away in 2003.

Leland and Barbara Edwards served together in Panama for almost twenty years. Leland was eight-years-old when he arrived in Panama, but he faithfully played his cornet in the services. He began preaching when he was fifteen and was appointed a Foursquare missionary in 1937, working mainly with the youth and directing camps in various parts of the country. Barbara arrived in Panama in 1941, and Leland and Barbara married in the Calle Q Church. They became the pastors of that church in 1945, and upon the retirement of Dr. Arthur Edwards in 1947, Leland was appointed supervisor for Panama and served in that position until January 1960. One of Barbara's ministries was leading people into the baptism with the Holy Spirit. They also served as missionaries in Chile during 1959. In 1960 they became members of the staff of the Foreign Missions Department at the international headquarters in Los Angeles, and served as director of Foursquare Missions International from 1965 to 1988. They reside in Lancaster, California.

Frank and Juventina Moncivaiz went to Panama in September 1931. They ministered with the Edwards family in Panama City, assisting in the work as it extended to other areas of the country. Later they moved to the interior city of Chitre, pastoring that church and opening other churches in the Herrera Province. In 1943 they were appointed to Mexico to start the Foursquare Church in that nation where they served until August 1975 when they retired and moved back to Los Angeles. Both are deceased.

Hazel Granvoll Shelley went to Panama in 1936 and was appointed as a Foursquare missionary in 1937, serving in Panama City and studying the Spanish language. A year later she moved to David to pioneer and establish the church in that city.

The work spread out into several areas of the Chiriquí Province. During World War II, Peyton Shelley, a cook with a unit of the U. S. Army near David, attended the David church. Hazel and Peyton were married after the war and served in the Chiriquí Province. Hazel went to be with the Lord in 1948, in the home of Leland and Barbara Edwards in Panama City. Peyton returned to the United States, where he pastored for several years. He is now deceased.

Elmer and Jean Darnall arrived in Panama in October 1944 and served in the ministry in Panama City. Later they moved to Colon during the furlough of the Donald Edwards family. They went to Santiago de Veraguas, where they ministered for a short time. Feeling the call to return to the United States to pastor, they left in October 1946. Later they started the work in Western Australia and ministered for several years in England and then, Hawaii. Jean is retired and ministers in Los Angeles; Elmer passed away in 2004.

Thaddeus and Helen Tuttle were appointed to Panama in January 1937, serving in the work in Panama City and later moving to the city of Penonome in the Cocle Province where they ministered under much persecution until June 1941. They returned to pastor churches in the United States. In 1945 they were appointed to Mexico to construct the church building in the city of Monterrey. In January 1947 they returned to Panama to pastor the Colon church and to supervise the work in the Colon Province. Thaddeus was the supervisor of the work in Panama for a year during the furlough of the Vinton Johnsons. They retired in 1968, but served a year in Honduras in 1969. He died in 1974, and Helen in 1982.

James Nicholls was sent to Panama in 1940, under special assignment. He was a radio engineer and there was a plan to establish a radio station in Panama for the Foursquare Church. It did not happen and he returned to the United States a few months later. He is now deceased.

Joseph and Virginia Knapp went to Panama in October 1944,

and after a few months in Panama City they moved to David, Chiriquí Province, during the furlough of Hazel and Peyton Shelley. In 1946 they were granted a visa to Colombia and left for that nation and started the work in the city of Barrancabermeja. They also served in Jamaica, Guatemala, and Puerto Rico. In 1975, they retired to live in California. Virginia died in 1985, and Joseph in 1993.

Mary Barkley went to Panama as a missionary from the Garr Auditorium in Charlotte, North Carolina, in 1946. She taught in the Bible institute and ministered in many of the churches in various parts of the country as well as in youth camps. One of her ministries was praying with people to receive the baptism of the Holy Spirit. She returned to Charlotte in November 1960, where she presently lives.

Mattie Sensabaugh went to Panama in December 1946, and after a time of orientation in Panama City, she moved to David, Chiriquí Province, and directed the work in that province until June 1952. In 1953 she moved to San Pedro Sula, Honduras, and pastored the church in that city; she also helped pioneer three other churches in the area. She retired in 1974, returning to the United States to live in Staunton, Virginia. She died in 1994.

Mary Frost started her missionary ministry in Panama in August 1946. She had been appointed to serve as a nurse in the children's home in Bucaramanga, Colombia but was unable to secure a visa. She applied for a visa in Panama and received it about a year later. During that year she served very faithfully in the Panama Church, wherever she could be of help. She died in Colombia after several fine years of serving the Colombia church.

Claude and Juanita Updike arrived in Panama in July 1948 and served in Panama until July 1952, assisting in the Calle Q Church, teaching in the Bible institute, and holding evangelistic campaigns in several areas of the country. During the following three years, they conducted evangelistic campaigns in several

Central American nations. In 1955 they moved to Guatemala and pioneered and established the Foursquare Church in that country. Juanita died in 1973, and Claude in 1988.

Vinton and Verna Johnson served in Panama from September 1949. After a few months of ministry in Panama City, they moved to David to lead the work in the Chiriquí Province. From there they moved to Yaviza in the Darien Province to begin the work of providing a written dialect of the Choco Indians and ministered in the churches in that area of Panama. Later they moved to Sambú, also in the Darien, and built the church and living quarters. In 1960 Vinton was appointed the supervisor of the Foursquare Church in Panama. In March 1966 the Johnsons were appointed to Argentina to supervise the work in that nation, returning to Panama in 1972 for one year of ministry. From 1973 to 1974, they were missionaries in Venezuela. Verna died in California in 1992, and Vinton in 1998.

Doris Cochran was appointed a missionary to serve in Colombia, but was unable to secure a visa in Los Angeles. She was sent to Panama to get the visa from the Colombian consulate. The visa was not granted, so she secured employment as a nurse in Gorgas Hospital, in the Canal Zone.

Robert and Alva Aguirre went to Panama in July 1954, and served in Panama City, teaching in the Bible school and in evangelistic meetings in various parts of the country. They also pastored the Calle Q Church when Leland and Barbara Edwards left to serve in Chile. In 1959 the Aguirres left Panama and went to Mexico for one year. The following year they went to Ecuador, ministering there until 1966. From 1968 to 1973, they were in charge of the work in Venezuela, and in 1974 they moved to Spain to start the Foursquare Church. They terminated their ministry as Foursquare missionaries in 1977. Robert died in California in 1991.

Carl and Rosemary Thompson arrived in Panama in October 1955 to pioneer and pastor a church for the Americans living in the Canal Zone. They started by renting the facility of the

Knights of Columbus in Balboa, and later the Canal Zone Government granted a lot in Diablo Heights on which they built the Diablo Heights Foursquare Church, called the Community Chapel. During their years on the isthmus, Rosemary worked as a secretary in a U. S. government office. The Thompsons retired in 1975 and moved to Texas. Carl died in 1984, and Rosemary in 1987.

Susano and Helen Soto went to Panama in August 1956 after having served for one year in Bolivia. They helped build the church building in Diablo Heights. Susano assisted in other church building constructions in Panama and also did much to assist in the making of the movie Life to Life, the story of the Foursquare Church in Panama. In 1958 he accepted employment with the Canal Zone Government and continued to assist national pastors on weekends. The Sotos returned to California from Panama, where Helen lives in retirement. Susano died several years ago.

Lucille Hicks went to Panama in June 1956 from Costa Rica, where she had served as a missionary for three years. She ministered in Colon and also Panama City in the Bible institutes and assisted in the church in Diablo Heights. She left Panama in April 1961 and now resides in Oregon, where she is serving in a local church.

Note: Nineteen of these missionaries, after a period of service in Panama, served as Foursquare missionaries in seventeen different countries. They also pioneered the Foursquare works in seven of those nations.

◄ To the Highways and Byways

D OWN THROUGH THE ages, people have settled along the shorelines of seas and rivers and in fertile agricultural lands. Trails were made by foot and animal traffic, establishing a means for communication and trade. With the coming of horse drawn vehicles and later automobiles and trucks, roads were made and people settled along these routes for the same reasons.

Shortly after my parents moved our family to Panama in 1928, the first major highway (two lanes) was laid into the interior; it was eventually paved a distance of about 165 miles. As time went on, the road extended to the city of David and then to the border with Costa Rica. During World War II, the highway was built across the isthmus, from the Atlantic to the Pacific. Again people moved along these thoroughfares, built their houses (often from native materials such as adobe, palm leaves for thatch, or handmade tiles for the roofs), and tilled small acreages to raise rice, bananas, various kinds of edible roots, corn, plantain, avocados, mangos, and papayas.

The spread of the gospel was mostly a spontaneous move of the Holy Spirit through the lives of the believers wanting to take the good news to family members and friends, many of them in need of the Great Physician. Meetings began in the little homes along the roads, or under the shade of large trees. From these, churches sprang up as people gave their hearts to the Lord. Their church buildings were very humble, built from the same materials that they used to build their houses.

Dad and Mother were very adept at both evangelizing and making disciples, teaching new converts the whole Word of God. It took time to start Bible institutes. The spread of the gospel went much faster than the training of workers: pastors, evangelists, and teachers. With the extension of the work, more supervision became necessary. This had to include teaching the fledgling leaders in these young, spontaneous church groups the Word of Life, the Bible. This meant that the missionaries had to spend time on the road using all kinds of transportation. Wherever the roads went, the missionaries could use the automobile. When the roads ended, the missionaries had to be more creative with modes of travel.

In the very early years of the Foursquare Church, missionaries either took their cars with them to the countries to which they were sent or, out of their own funds, purchased a local secondhand vehicle. In later years that changed, and the missions department provided new vehicles. Dad shipped our car to Panama when we went in 1928. It was a 1925 Studebaker touring car; it had a solid roof and could be closed in on each side with sliding windows from the back to the front. It was called a California Top, and was the only car in the country of its kind.

As I grew older and became involved in ministry, I used all kinds of transportation to get to destinations for ministry: public buses, trains, boats, light airplanes, and commercial airlines, mostly DC–3s. Getting to some churches meant hiking for many miles, often over centuries-old trails from past Indian civilizations. What kind of boats did we use? On Gatun Lake (part of the Panama Canal), we traveled in launches that carried passengers and cargo.

Gatun Lake was created during the construction of the Panama Canal. In fact, it was the largest artificial lake in the world until the building of Hoover Dam, which created Lake Meade. Its water covered vast areas of heavily wooded jungles. In many areas of the lake, away from the main channels, the tops of the trees stood out of the water. This left large areas of stumps that were visible above the water, and others not visible, lying just below the surface. Travel could be very dangerous.

One of the church buildings, which had been constructed of secondhand lumber, was located on the banks of the Gatun

Lake in the village of Caño Quebrado, where there were banana farms. To get to Caño Quebrado it was necessary to go across the Gatun Lake, part of the Panama Canal waterway. My dad purchased an old metal lifeboat from U. S. Navy surplus and put it on the vacant lot next to the house we rented in Panama City. He and my brother completely repaired the steel hull and redesigned the stern, so an outboard motor could be mounted on it. The general supervisor of the Foursquare Church in the United States, Rev. Charles Rosendahl, had been previously employed by the Indian Motorcycle Company. In 1930 that company began making outboard motors. At his request, the Indian Motorcycle Company made a donation of an outboard motor to the ministry of the Foursquare Church in Panama. This provided the means to cross the lake, a trip of about two hours, to assist the work in Caño Quebrado.

In the early part of our ministry together, Barb and I had traveled across the lake to the church in Caño Quebrado for a large baptismal service at the lake's edge. In the very late afternoon, we left and headed for home. In the narrow channel leading out of Caño Quebrado, the pilot of the small launch missed a turn, and we plowed into the stumps. The boat went up on a large stump, which broke through the bottom of the boat. Water began pouring in. It was dark, and the passengers became very frightened. Those waters were known for large crocodiles. Fortunately for us, some men on the back of a barge that was being towed a short distance from us heard our cries for help. The launch that was towing the barge came back after us. It and its barge were going the opposite direction from where we wanted to go, but we were glad to get on board and spend the night in another town. We returned to our car the next day.

To go to the Darien Province, which borders Colombia, all travel had to be on water. We traveled on wooden cargo boats powered by diesel engines, which carried heavy loads, mostly plantains, to the market in Panama City. These small wooden freighters averaged about sixty feet in length and about eighteen feet in width. We had to navigate on the open ocean for about 120 miles, and then up the Tuira and Chucunaque Rivers. There were Foursquare churches along the banks of these rivers, and, in spite of the danger involved, we were happy to visit the congregations to provide both teaching and encouragement.

One of our young national pastors and his wife had started a work in Punta de Chame. It was a village at the end of a small peninsula, about fifty miles up the coast from Panama City. The only way to get there was by sailboat. We had accepted the invitation of the pastors to visit that young congregation in Punta de Chame. We took four of the Crusaders from our church, young people who would help in the meetings. We sailed from Panama City at night and arrived at our destination the next day before noon. The breeze was steady and the sea was calm. As I recall, we had a wonderful time with the congregation. For the return trip, we boarded the same vessel. It was loaded with charcoal; producing charcoal from the mangroves was the livelihood of Punta de Chame. The hold was completely packed full. We started our return voyage in late afternoon. But by the next morning we had only gone a short distance. There we sat out on the sea, no wind and the water as smooth as glass. All of a sudden, the skies darkened and, in no time, a storm hit us with very heavy winds and rain. We earnestly prayed for help; the situation was very dangerous.

In a short while a torpedo boat of the U. S. Army approached us but then went on. We continued waving our hands and yelling, and the boat returned. The pilot brought the boat alongside and took us all on. We were taken into the galley where some of the crew fed us wonderful ham sandwiches and gave us good water to drink. They took us to the dock in Balboa Harbor, and from there we caught a bus back to the church.

After World War II, we purchased two Dodge pickup trucks from U. S. Army surplus. On the bed of each we built covers and benches. To help us in our efforts to open more meeting places along the interior highway, we enlisted the help of national workers, some of them Bible institute students. We would load them into the pickup trucks on Saturday afternoons and drop them off by twos in different towns. The various pairs would hold services Saturday evening and Sunday morning; then the drivers picked them up Sunday afternoon and drove them back to Panama City. In summertime, which was the dry season, during the schools' vacation times, a similar method was used to spread workers along the highway in various towns where daily vacation Bible schools were conducted.

One of the men, William Bowman, who attended the Calle Q Church, had bought a third interest in a PT–19, a primary trainer used during World War II. The plane had two open cockpits. Since the other two owners seldom used the airplane, this man enjoyed using the aircraft to help in spreading the gospel. Several times, when our church was holding large outdoor meetings in the interior towns, I would fly with him and drop printed invitations by the thousands over the places where the meetings were to be held. We would also drop tracts. Also, we were able to fly to conferences and conventions in every part of Panama.

As I look back at the amount of time I spent "getting there and back home," I am amazed at two things: that I am still alive (some of those trips were downright dangerous!), and how daring I was to even enjoy the trip. Chalk it up either to my being young and foolhardy, or to being willing to do what it took to see that people heard the gospel. All I can say is that those trips were some of the most exciting times of my life.